Fairy Tale Charted Designs

by Jeanne M. Warth

DOVER PUBLICATIONS, INC., NEW YORK

Published in Canada by General Publishing Company, Ltd., 30 Lesmill Road, Don Mills, Toronto, Ontario.
Published in the United Kingdom by Constable and Company, Ltd., 10 Orange Street, London WC2H 7EG.

Fairy Tale Charted Designs is a new work, first published by Dover Publications, Inc., in 1986.

Manufactured in the United States of America
Dover Publications, Inc., 31 East 2nd Street, Mineola, N.Y. 11501

Library of Congress Cataloging-in-Publication Data

Warth, Jeanne M.
  Fairy tale charted designs.

  (Dover needlework series)
  1. Needlework—Patterns.   2. Fairy tales.   I. Title.   II. Series.
TT753.W38   1986   746.3041   86-13575
ISBN 0-486-25195-0 (pbk.)

INTRODUCTION

From earliest childhood, fairy tales and fables are part of our lives. Cinderella and her prince, Goldilocks and the Three Bears, the Hare and the Tortoise—all are familiar friends to children and adults alike. This collection presents characters from fifteen favorite tales, including *Rapunzel, Puss in Boots, The City Mouse and the Country Mouse, The Emperor's New Clothes* and *Hansel and Gretel*.

In addition to individual motifs and motifs surrounded by borders, charts are given for four large fairy-tale houses—Cinderella's house, Grandma's house from *Little Red Riding Hood*, the brick house from *The Three Little Pigs* and the bears' house from *Goldilocks and the Three Bears*. The chart for each of these houses is printed over four pages in the book.

The houses were originally designed for needlepoint and are color-keyed to Paternayan Persian yarn. The larger areas of color are outlined and the color numbers written in. Scattered stitches are indicated by symbols. With the chart for each house, there is a chart listing which colors are used and where they are used. On both *Cinderella* and *Goldilocks and the Three Bears*, certain details are "over-stitched" with long straight stitches after the other stitching is completed. A separate chart is given for these details.

The remaining charts are color-keyed to both Paternayan Persian yarn (abbreviated PAT. in the color keys) and DMC six-strand embroidery floss. Larger areas of color are outlined and identified by letter, while scattered stitches are identified by symbols.

The wonderfully detailed fairy-tale houses make charming pictures for a child's room, and the smaller designs can be used to create pillows and pictures, latch hook rugs, crocheted afghans and knitted sweaters. No matter how the designs are used, they are sure to delight anyone who receives them.

NEEDLEPOINT

Materials

1. **Needles**. A blunt tapestry needle with a rounded tip and an elongated eye. The needle must clear the hole of the canvas without spreading the threads. For No. 10 canvas, a No. 18 needle works best.

2. **Canvas**. There are two distinct types of needlepoint canvas: single-mesh (mono canvas) and double-mesh (Penelope canvas). Single-mesh canvas, the more common of the two, is easier on the eyes as the spaces are slightly larger. Double-mesh canvas has two horizontal and two vertical threads forming each mesh. The latter is a very stable canvas on which the threads stay securely in place as the work progresses. Canvas is available in many sizes, from 5 mesh-per-inch to 18 mesh-per-inch, and even smaller. The number of mesh-per-inch will, of course, determine the dimensions of the finished needlepoint project. A 60 square × 120 square chart will measure 12″ × 24″ on 5 mesh-to-the-inch canvas, 5″ × 10″ on 12 mesh-to-the-inch canvas. The most common canvas size is 10 to the inch.

3. **Yarns**. Persian, crewel and tapestry yarns all work well on needlepoint canvas.

Preparing to Work

Allow 1″ to 1½″ blank canvas all around. Bind the raw edges of the canvas with masking tape or machine-stitched double-fold bias tape.

There are few hard-and-fast rules on where to begin the design. It is best to complete the main motif, then fill the background as the last step.

For any guidelines you wish to draw on the canvas, take care that your marking medium is waterproof. Nonsoluble inks, acrylic paints thinned with water so as not to clog the mesh, and waterproof felt-tip pens all work well. If unsure, experiment on a scrap of canvas.

When working with multiple strands (such as Persian yarn) always separate (strand) the yarn before beginning to stitch. This one small step allows for better coverage of the canvas. When you need more than one piece of yarn in the needle, use separate strands and do not double the yarn. For example: If you need two strands of 3-ply Persian yarn, use two separated strands. Yarn has a nap (just as fabrics do) and can be felt to be smoother in one direction than the other. Always work with the nap (the smooth side) pointing down.

For 5 mesh-to-the-inch canvas, use six strands of 3-ply yarn; for 10 mesh-to-the-inch canvas, use three strands of 3-ply yarn.

Stitching

Cut yarn lengths 18" long. Begin needlepoint by holding about 1" of loose yarn on the wrong side of the work and working the first several stitches over the loose end to secure it. To end a piece of yarn, run it under several completed stitches on the wrong side of the work.

There are hundreds of needlepoint stitch variations, but tent stitch is universally considered to be *the* needlepoint stitch. The most familiar versions of tent stitch are half-cross stitch, continental stitch and basket-weave stitch.

Half-cross stitch (*Diagram 1*) is worked from left to right. The canvas is then turned around and the return row is again stitched from left to right. Holding the needle vertically, bring 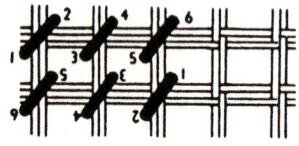 DIAGRAM 1

it to the front of the canvas through the hole that will be the bottom of the first stitch. Keep the stitches loose for minimum distortion and good coverage. Half-cross stitch is best worked on a double-mesh canvas.

Continental stitch (*Diagram 2*) begins in the upper right-hand corner and is worked from right to left. The needle is slanted and always brought out a mesh ahead. The resulting stitch appears as a half-cross stitch on the front and as a slanting stitch on the back. When the row is complete, turn the canvas around to work the return row, continuing to stitch from right to left.

DIAGRAM 2

Basket-weave stitch (*Diagram 3*) begins in the upper right-hand corner with four continental stitches (two stitches worked horizontally across the top and two placed directly below the first stitch). Work diagonal rows, the first slanting up and across the canvas from right to left, and the next down and across from left to right. Moving down the canvas from left to right, the needle is in a vertical position; working in the opposite direction, the needle is horizontal. The rows interlock, creating a basket-weave pattern on the wrong side. If the stitch is not done properly, a faint ridge will show where the pattern was interrupted. On basket-weave stitch, always stop working in the middle of a row, rather than at the end, so that you will know in which direction you were working.

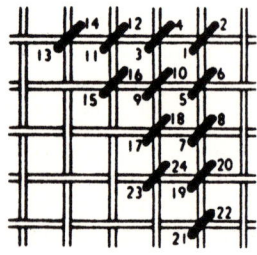

DIAGRAM 3

COUNTED CROSS-STITCH

Materials

1. **Needles.** A small blunt tapestry needle, No. 24 or No. 26.

2. **Fabric.** Evenweave linen, cotton, wool or synthetic fabrics all work well. The most popular fabrics are aida cloth, linen and hardanger cloth. Cotton aida is most commonly available in 18 threads-per-inch, 14 threads-per-inch and 11 threads-per-inch (14-count is the most popular size). Evenweave linen comes in a variety of threads-per-inch. To work cross-stitch on linen involves a slightly different technique (see page 5). Thirty thread-per-inch linen will result in a stitch about the same size as 14-count aida. Hardanger cloth has 22 threads to the inch and is available in cotton or linen. The amount of fabric needed depends on the size of the cross-stitch design. To determine yardage, divide the number of stitches in the design by the thread-count of the fabric. For example: If a design 112 squares wide by 140 squares deep is worked on a 14-count fabric, divide 112 by 14 (= 8), and 140 by 14 (= 10). The design will measure 8" × 10". The same design worked on 22-count fabric measures about 5" × 6½".

3. **Threads and Yarns.** Six-strand embroidery floss, crewel wool, Danish Flower Thread, pearl cotton or metallic threads all work well for cross-stitch. Crewel wool works well on evenweave wool fabric. Danish Flower Thread is a thicker thread with a matte finish, one strand equaling two of embroidery floss.

4. **Embroidery Hoop.** A wooden or plastic 4", 5" or 6" round or oval hoop with a screw-type tension adjuster works best for cross-stitch.

5. **Scissors.** A pair of sharp embroidery scissors is essential to all embroidery.

Preparing to Work

To prevent raveling, either whip stitch or machine-stitch the outer edges of the fabric.

Locate the exact center of the chart. Establish the center of the fabric by folding it in half first vertically, then horizontally. The center stitch of the chart falls where the creases of the fabric meet. Mark the fabric center with a basting thread.

It is best to begin cross-stitch at the top of the design. To establish the top, count the squares up from the center of the chart, and the corresponding number of holes up from the center of the fabric.

Place the fabric tautly in the embroidery hoop, for tension makes it easier to push the needle through the holes without piercing the fibers. While working continue to retighten the fabric as necessary.

When working with multiple strands (such as embroidery floss) always separate (strand) the thread before beginning to stitch. This one small step allows for better coverage of the fabric. When you need more than one thread in the needle, use separate strands and do not double the thread. (For example: If you need four strands, use four separated strands.) Thread has a nap (just as fabrics do) and can be felt to be smoother in one direction than the other. Always work with the nap (the smooth side) pointing down.

For 14-count aida and 30-count linen, work with two

strands of six-strand floss. For more texture, use more thread; for a flatter look, use less thread.

Embroidery

To begin, fasten the thread with a waste knot and hold a short length of thread on the underside of the work, anchoring it with the first few stitches (*Diagram 4*). When the thread end is securely in place, clip the knot.

DIAGRAM 4
Reverse side of work

To stitch, push the needle up through a hole in the fabric, cross the thread intersection (or square) on a left-to-right diagonal (*Diagram 5*). Half the stitch is now completed.

DIAGRAM 5

Next, cross back, right to left, forming an X (*Diagram 6*).

DIAGRAM 6

DIAGRAM 7

Work all the same color stitches on one row, then cross back, completing the X's (*Diagram 7*).

Some needleworkers prefer to cross each stitch as they come to it. This method also works, but be sure all of the top stitches are slanted in the same direction. Isolated stitches must be crossed as they are worked. Vertical stitches are crossed as shown in *Diagram 8*.

DIAGRAM 8

At the top, work horizontal rows of a single color, left to right. This method allows you to go from an unoccupied space to an occupied space (working from an empty hole to a filled one), making ruffling of the floss less likely. Holes are used more than once, and all stitches "hold hands" unless a space is indicated on the chart. Hold the work upright throughout (do not turn as with many needlepoint stitches).

When carrying the thread from one area to another, run the needle under a few stitches on the wrong side. Do not carry thread across an open expanse of fabric as it will be visible from the front when the project is completed.

Embroidery on Linen. Working on linen requires a slightly different technique. While evenweave linen is remarkably regular, there are always a few thick or thin threads. To keep the stitches even, cross-stitch is worked over two threads in each direction (*Diagram 9*).

DIAGRAM 9

Embroidery on Gingham. Gingham and other checked fabrics can be used for cross-stitch. Using the fabric as a guide, work the stitches from corner to corner of each check.

Embroidery on Uneven-Weave Fabrics. If you wish to work cross-stitch on an uneven-weave fabric, baste a lightweight Penelope needlepoint canvas to the material. The design can then be stitched by working the cross-stitch over the double mesh of the canvas. When working in this manner, take care not to catch the threads of the canvas in the embroidery. After the cross-stitch is completed, remove the basting threads. With tweezers remove first the vertical threads, one strand at a time, of the needlepoint canvas, then the horizontal threads.

KNITTING

Charted designs can be worked into stockinette stitch as you are knitting, or they can be embroidered with duplicate stitch when the knitting is complete. For the former, wind the different colors of yarn on bobbins and work in the same manner as in Fair Isle knitting. A few quick Fair Isle tips: (1) Always bring up the new color yarn from under the dropped color to prevent holes. (2) Carry the color not in use loosely across the wrong side of the work, but not more than three or four stitches without twisting the yarns. If a color is not in use for more than seven or eight stitches, it is usually best to drop that color yarn and rejoin a new bobbin when the color is again needed.

CROCHET

There are a number of ways in which charts can be used for crochet. Among them are:

Single Crochet

Single crochet is often seen worked in multiple colors. When changing colors, always pick up the new color for the last yarn-over of the old color. The color not in use can be carried loosely across the back of the work for a few stitches, or you can work the single crochet over the unused color. The latter method makes for a neater appearance on the wrong side, but sometimes the old color peeks through the stitches. This method can also be applied to half-double crochet and double crochet, but keep in mind that the longer stitches will distort the design.

Filet Crochet

This technique is nearly always worked from charts and uses only one color thread. The result is a solid-color piece with the design filled in and the background left as an open mesh. Care must be taken in selecting the design, as the longer stitch causes distortion.

Afghan Crochet

The most common method here is cross-stitch worked over the afghan stitch. Complete the afghan crochet project. Then, following the chart for color placement, work cross-stitch over the squares of crochet.

OTHER CHARTED METHODS

Latch hook, Assisi embroidery, beading, cross-stitch on needlepoint canvas (a European favorite) and lace net embroidery are among the other needlework methods worked from charts.

EMBROIDERED DETAILS

Straight stitch or French knots are used to stitch the details on several of the designs.

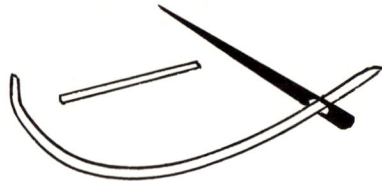

Straight stitch

French knot

The Emperor's New Clothes

LETTER/ SYMBOL	COLOR	PAT. #	DMC #	LETTER/ SYMBOL	COLOR	PAT. #	DMC #
W/⊡	White	260	—	☒	Gold	744	677
P/⊙	Violet	300	552	⊟	Pale Pink	875	948
S	Light Brown	463	841	⊟	Pink	932	899
⊞	Medium Brown	462	839	⊿	Red	950	321
F	Flesh	494	712	☑	Assorted colors	—	—
B/⊙	Blue	541	312				

Rapunzel

LETTER/ SYMBOL	COLOR	PAT. #	DMC #
R	Charcoal Gray	221	844
⊿	Dark Gray	200	645
M	Medium Gray	202	647
⊡	Light Gray	256	762
⊡	White	260	—
⊙	Blue	583	518
⊟	Dark Green	682	910
⊞	Medium Green	684	912
G	Light Green	687	955
⊟	Dark Yellow	713	726
Y	Yellow	714	727
⊙	Pale Pink	875	948
—	*Pink	934	761
F	Pale Flesh	948	712

*Stitch mouth in straight stitch, over completed stitches.

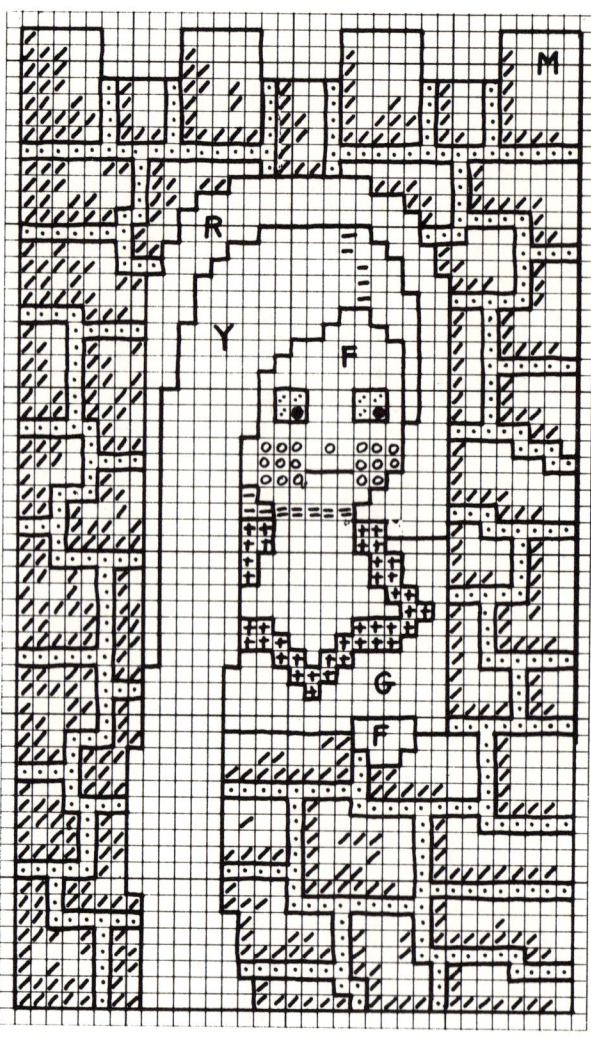

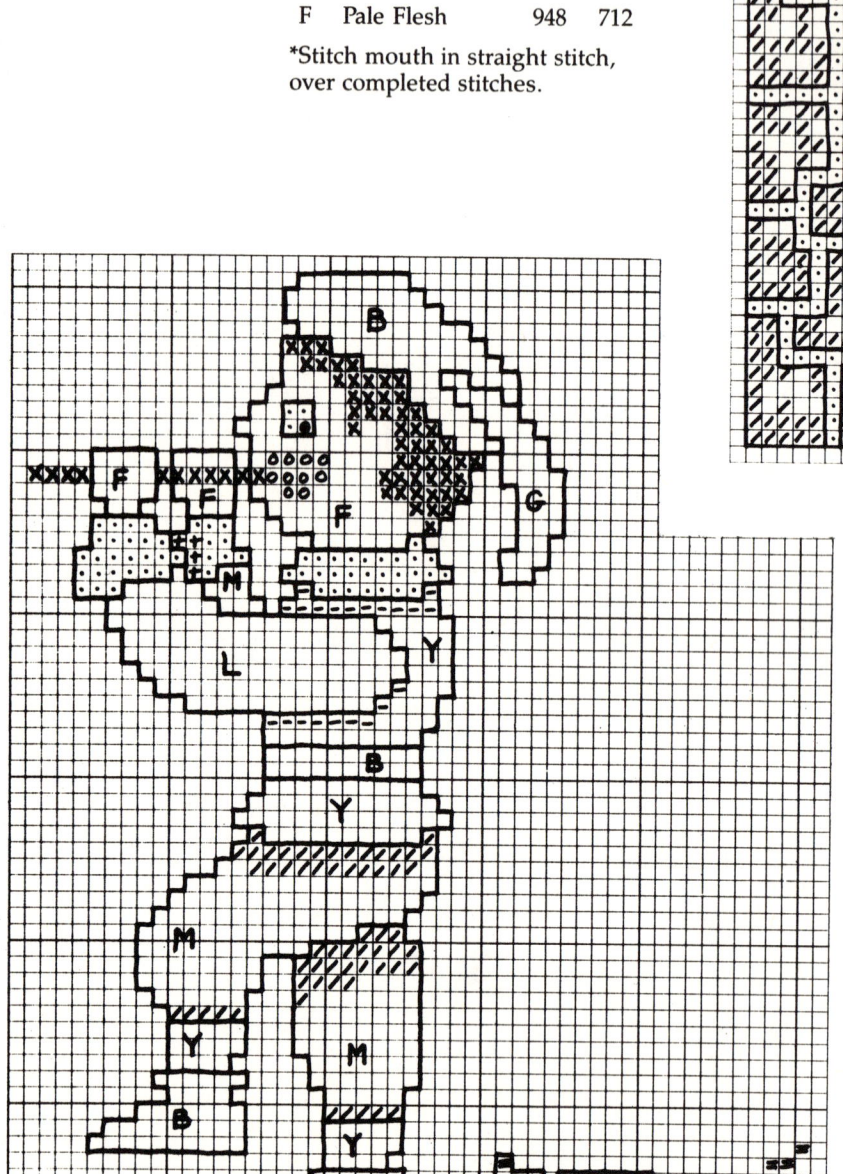

The Pied Piper of Hamelin

LETTER/ SYMBOL	COLOR	PAT. #	DMC #
⊟	Dark Gray	202	646
R	Light Gray	203	648
⊡	White	260	—
⊠	Dark Brown	411	801
B	Brown	412	435
F	Flesh	494	712
⊿	Dark Blue	551	824
M/⊙	Medium Blue	552	826
L	Light Blue	553	813
⊞	Pale Blue	556	828
G	Green	698	907
⊟	Dark Yellow	726	725
Y	Yellow	727	726
⊙	Pale Pink	875	948

Eyes

Puss in Boots

LETTER/ SYMBOL	COLOR	PAT. #	DMC #
	*Charcoal Gray	221	844
⊙	Dark Gray	201	645
☑	Gray	203	648
W/⊡	White	260	—
☒	Dark Brown	452	610
Q/☑	Medium Brown	453	612
B	Light Brown	455	613
G	Green	693	3347
⊡	Light Green	633	704
⊟	Gold	725	783
M	Light Gold	727	726
⊞	Dark Red	940	815
R	Red	941	321
⊙	Light Pink	933	791

*Stitch vertical lines in straight stitch, over completed eyes as shown.

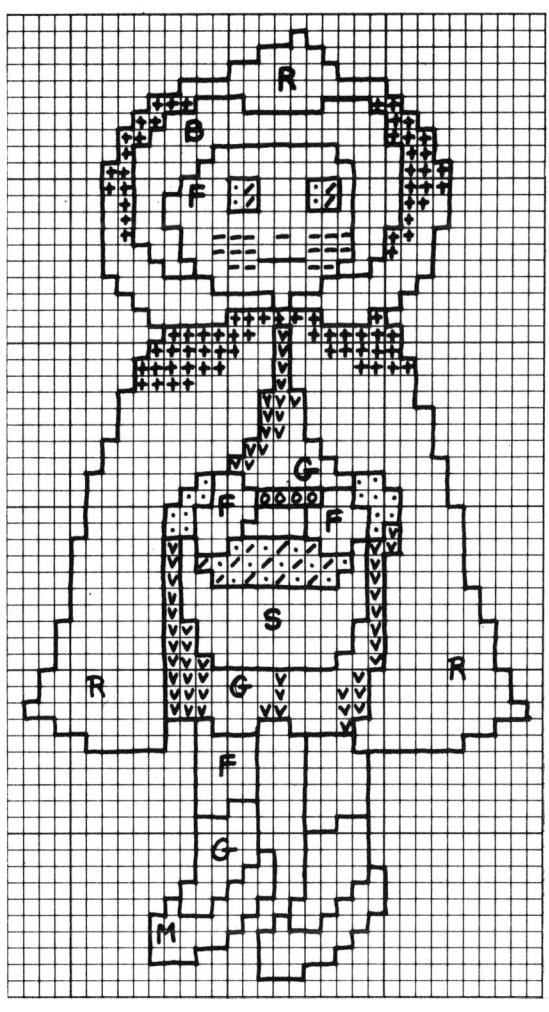

Little Red Riding Hood

LETTER/ SYMBOL	COLOR	PAT. #	DMC #
M	Black	220	310
⊡	White	260	—
B	Brown	403	436
☑	Blue	543	826
☑	Light Green	684	912
G	Pale Green	687	955
S/⊙	Straw	753	676
⊞	Dark Red	840	816
R	Red	970	321
—	*Pink	844	761
⊟	Pale Pink	875	948
F	Pale Flesh	948	712

*Stitch mouth in straight stitch, over completed stitches.

Goldilocks and the Three Bears

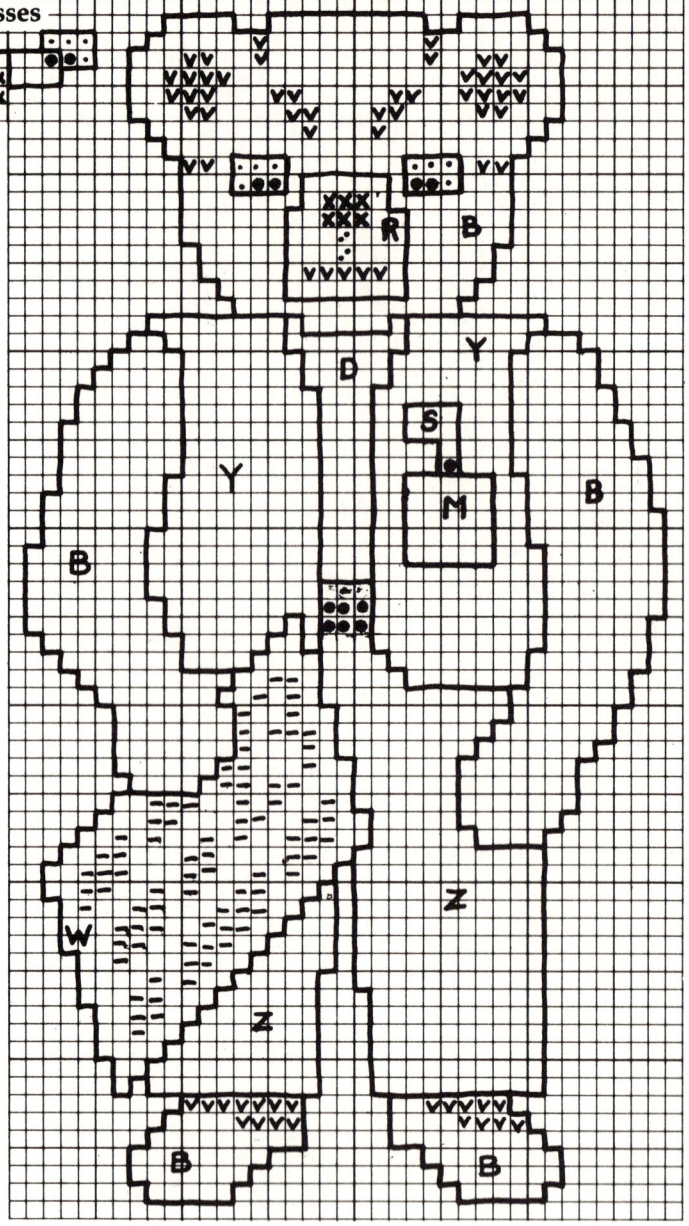

Eyeglasses

Papa Bear

LETTER/ SYMBOL	COLOR	PAT. #	DMC #
⊡	Black	220	310
⊟	Light Gray	213	415
W/⊡	White	260	—
⊠	Dark Brown	431	801
D/☑	Medium Brown	432	433
B/⊡	Light Brown	434	435
R	Light Beige	405	613
M	Dark Yellow	711	725
Y	*Yellow	712	726
S	Dark Rust	861	301
Z	Red	940	498

*Stitch eyeglasses in straight stitch, over completed eyes as shown.

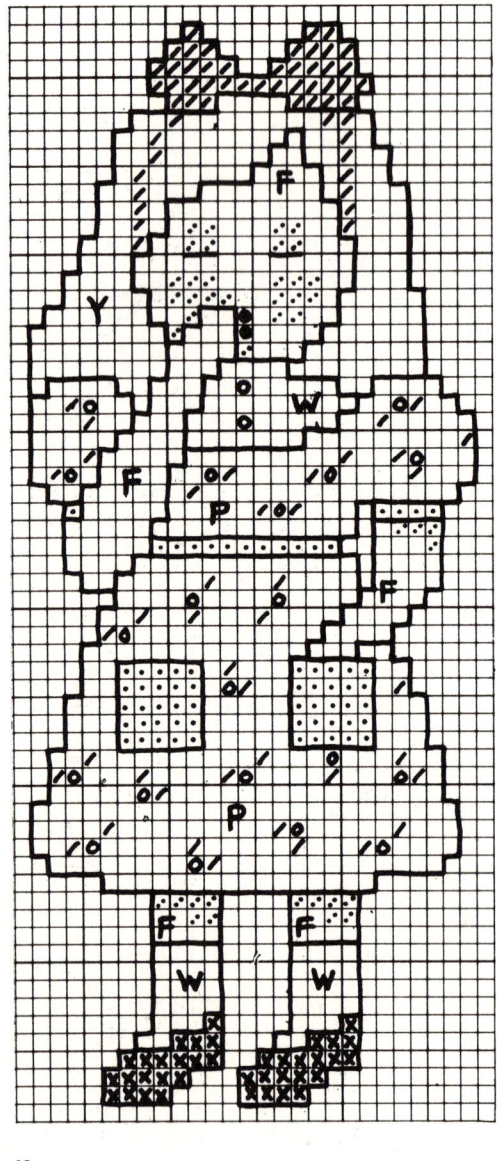

Goldilocks

LETTER/ SYMBOL	COLOR	PAT. #	DMC #
⊠	Black	220	310
W/⊡	White	260	
—	*Light Coffee Brown	424	680
◪	Green	683	911
Y	Yellow	713	726
⊡	Medium Flesh	875	948
F	Pale Flesh	948	712
◉	Dark Pink	943	309
◼	Medium Rusty Pink	932	899
P	Light Pink	945	776

*Stitch horizontal lines below eyes in straight stitch, over completed stitches.

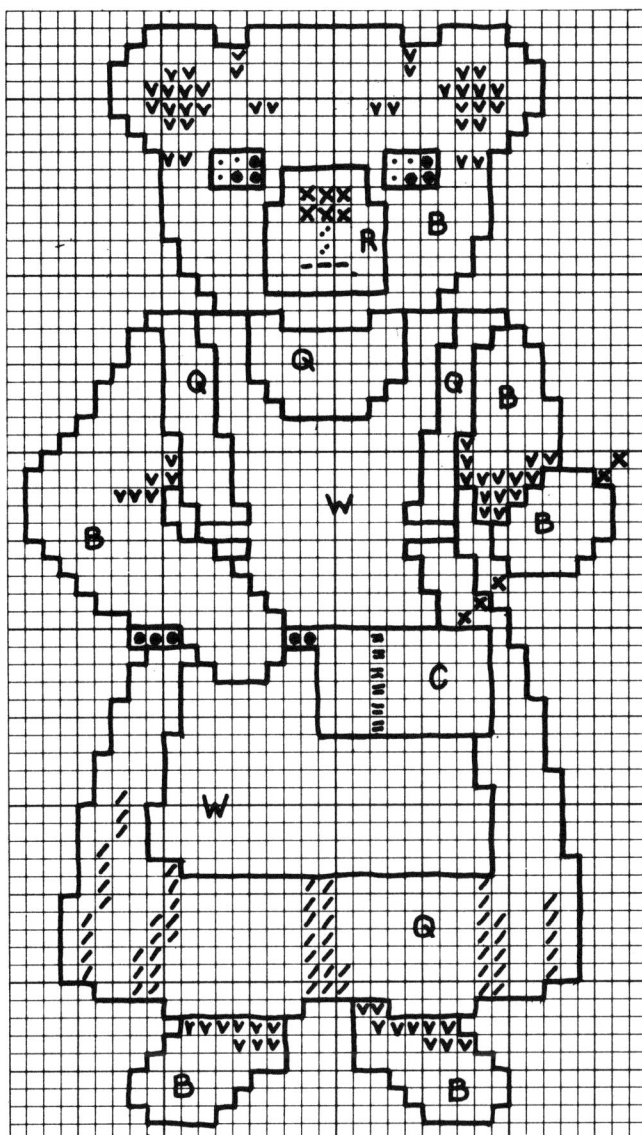

Mama Bear

LETTER/ SYMBOL	COLOR	PAT. #	DMC #
⊙	Black	220	310
W/·	White	260	—
☒	Dark Brown	431	801
☑	Medium Brown	432	433
B/⊡	Light Brown	434	435
R	Light Beige	405	613
⊿	Dark Green	632	904
Q	Medium Green	633	906
⊟	Yellow	713	726
C	Copper	884	402
⊟	Rusty Pink	933	761

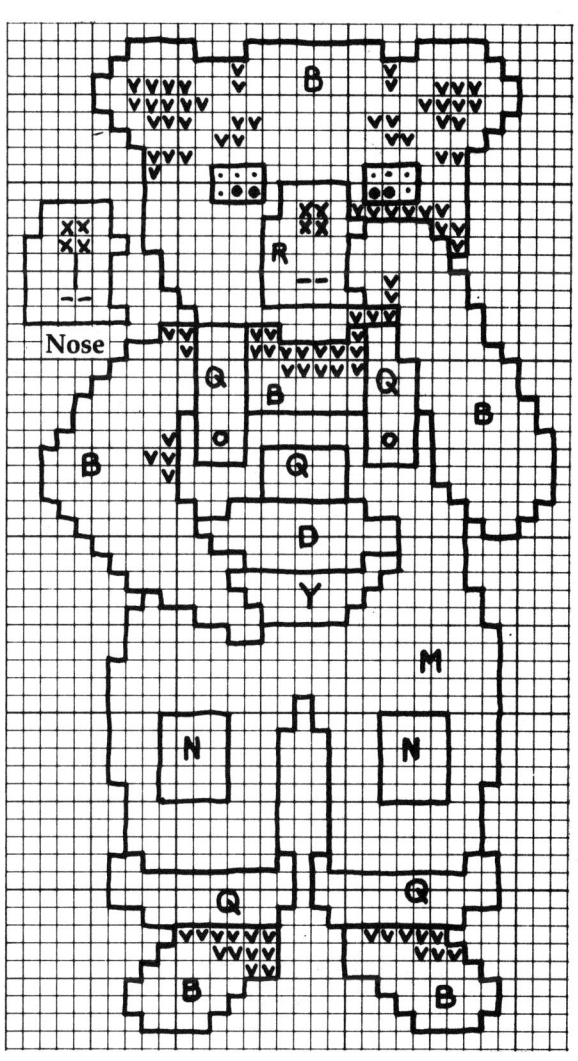

Baby Bear

LETTER/ SYMBOL	COLOR	PAT. #	DMC #
⊙	Black	220	310
·	White	260	—
☒	Dark Brown	431	801
☑	Medium Brown	432	433
B/ ⌐	*Light Brown	434	435
R	Light Beige	405	613
M	Blue	543	334
Q	Light Blue	545	775
D	Dark Yellow Orange	771	972
Y/⊡	Yellow Orange	772	973
N	Red	950	817
⊟	Medium Rusty Pink	932	758

*Stitch vertical line in backstitch over completed nose.

The Little Red Hen

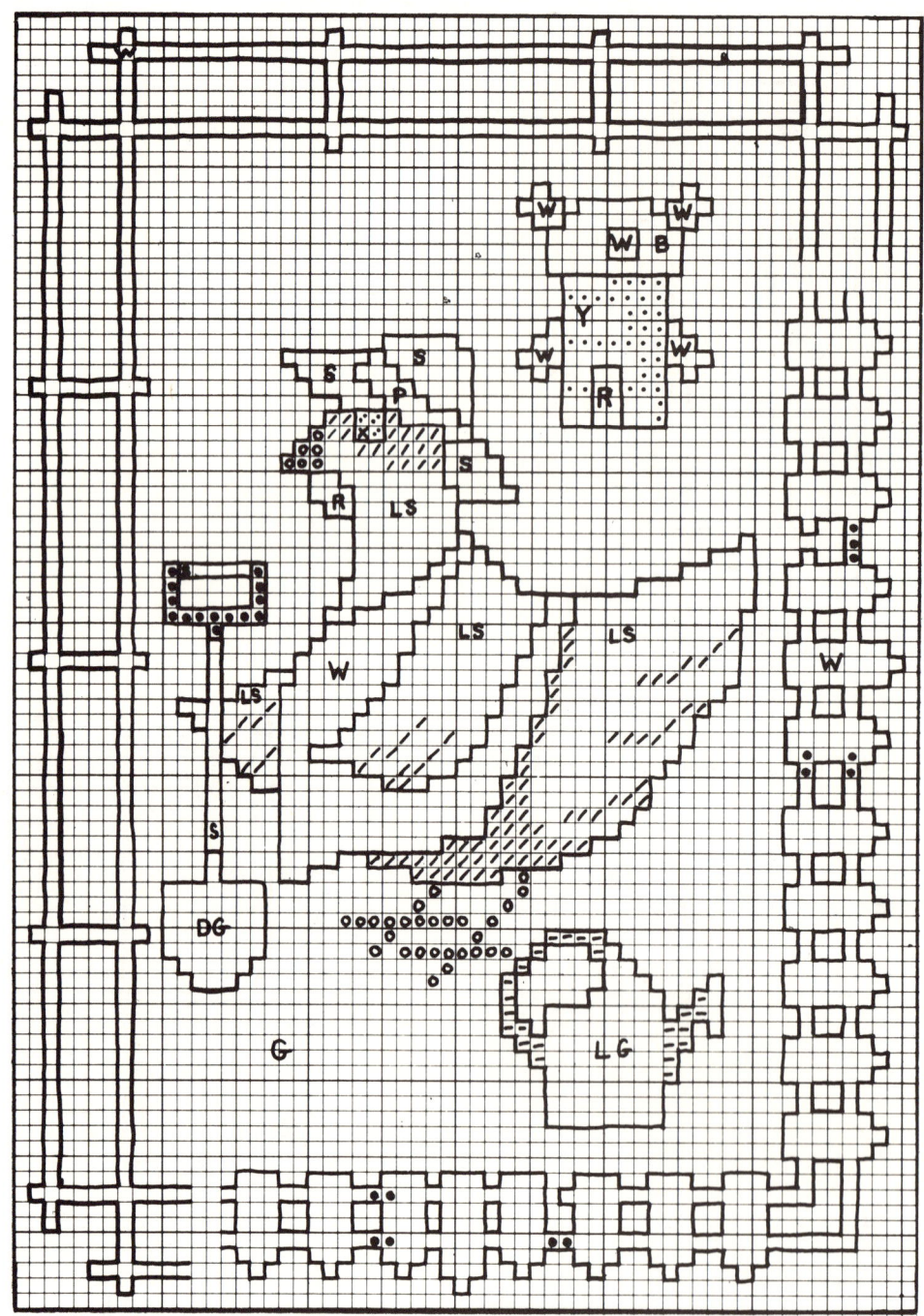

Little Red Hen with Two Borders

LETTER/ SYMBOL	COLOR	PAT. #	DMC #	LETTER/ SYMBOL	COLOR	PAT. #	DMC #
DG/▣	Dark Gray	210	413	▫	Dark Yellow	711	783
⊟	Medium Gray	211	414	Y	Yellow	712	726
LG	Light Gray	212	415	▱	Medium Rust	721	976
W/▯	White	260	—	LS	Light Rust	723	977
B	Blue	552	797	S	Straw	744	834
G/▨	Green	633	3348	R	Red	972	350
▣	Light Orange	702	743	P	Pink	904	893

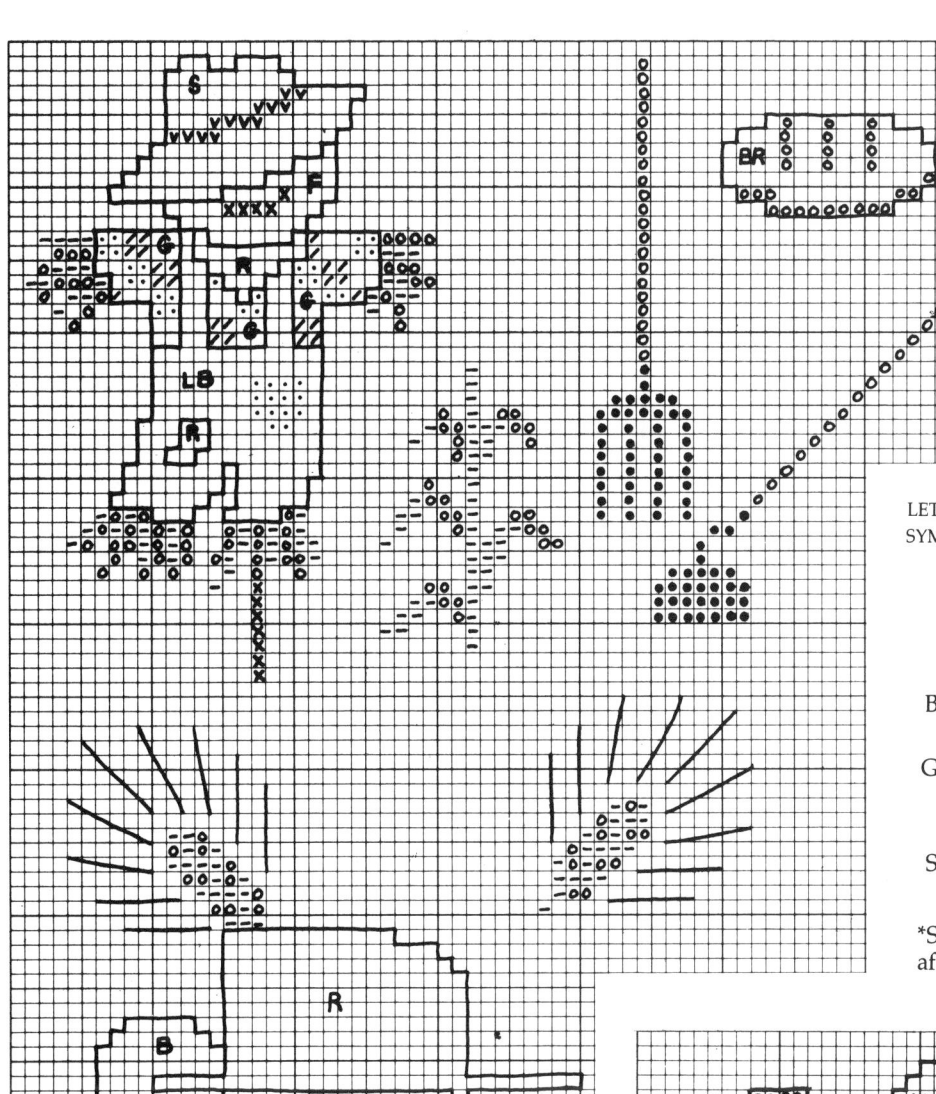

Scarecrow, Tools, Wheelbarrow, Bread and Wheat

LETTER/ SYMBOL	COLOR	PAT. #	DMC #
⊡	Dark Gray	210	413
☒	Medium Brown	423	434
BR	Light Brown	412	436
F	Flesh	494	543
B/⊡	Medium Blue	552	798
LB	Light Blue	554	800
G/☑	Green	632	907
⁄	Yellow	713	726
−	Dark Straw	743	729
S/Ⓞ	*Medium Straw	745	677
R	Red	971	321

*Stitch lines of wheat in straight stitch, after all other stitching is complete.

Little Red Hen

LETTER/ SYMBOL	COLOR	PAT. #	DMC #
⊡	White	260	—
☒	Light Brown	412	436
B	Light Blue	555	828
⊞	Green	693	3347
Ⓞ	Light Orange	702	743
⁄	Medium Rust	721	976
S	Light Rust	723	977
⊡	Dark Straw	742	729
M/⊡	Light Straw	745	677
R	Red	972	350

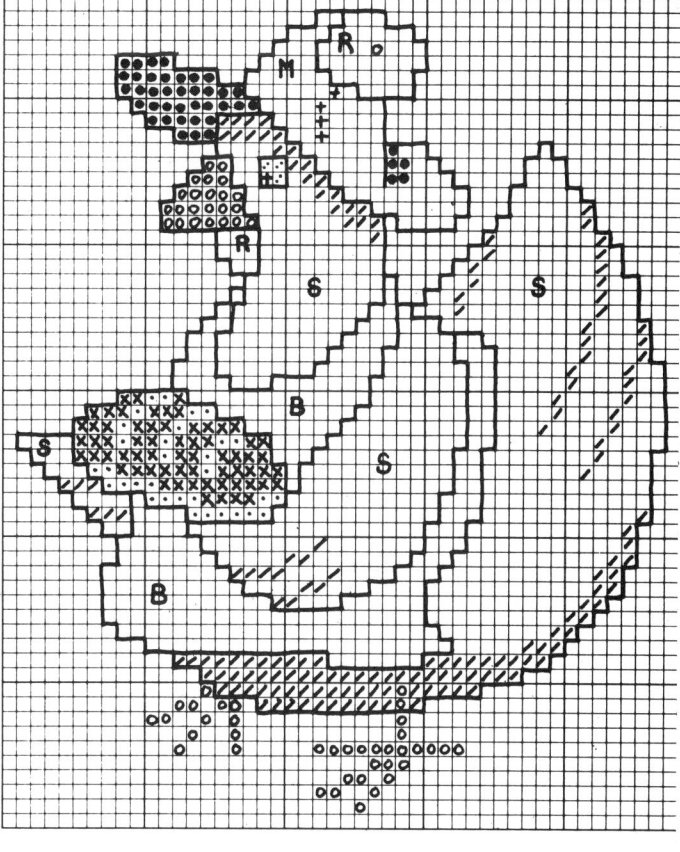

The Ugly Duckling

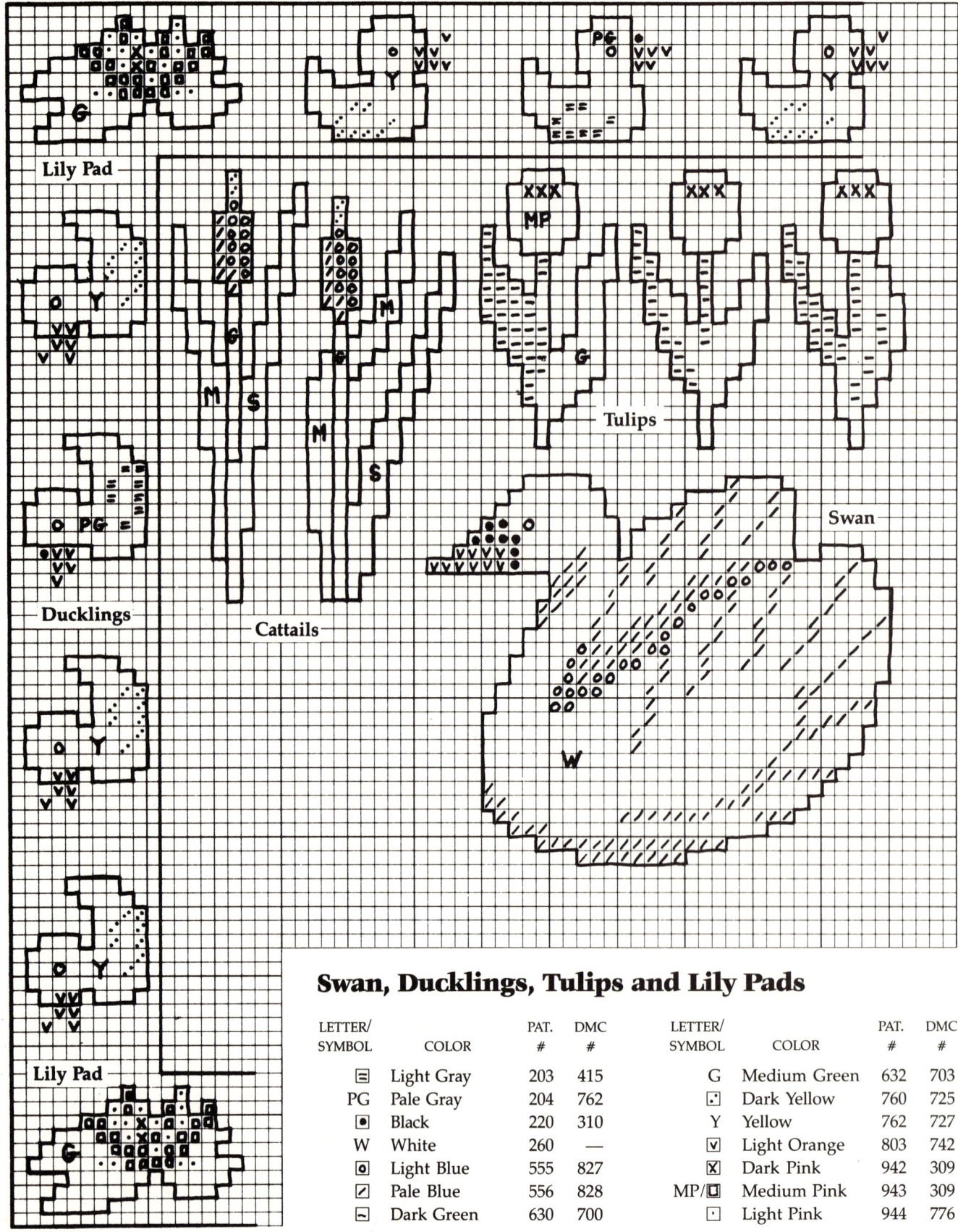

Lily Pad

Lily Pad

Ducklings

Cattails

Tulips

Swan

Lily Pad

Swan, Ducklings, Tulips and Lily Pads

LETTER/ SYMBOL	COLOR	PAT. #	DMC #	LETTER/ SYMBOL	COLOR	PAT. #	DMC #
⊟	Light Gray	203	415	G	Medium Green	632	703
PG	Pale Gray	204	762	⊡	Dark Yellow	760	725
⊙	Black	220	310	Y	Yellow	762	727
W	White	260	—	⊻	Light Orange	803	742
⊙	Light Blue	555	827	⊠	Dark Pink	942	309
⊘	Pale Blue	556	828	MP/⊡	Medium Pink	943	309
⊟	Dark Green	630	700	⊡	Light Pink	944	776

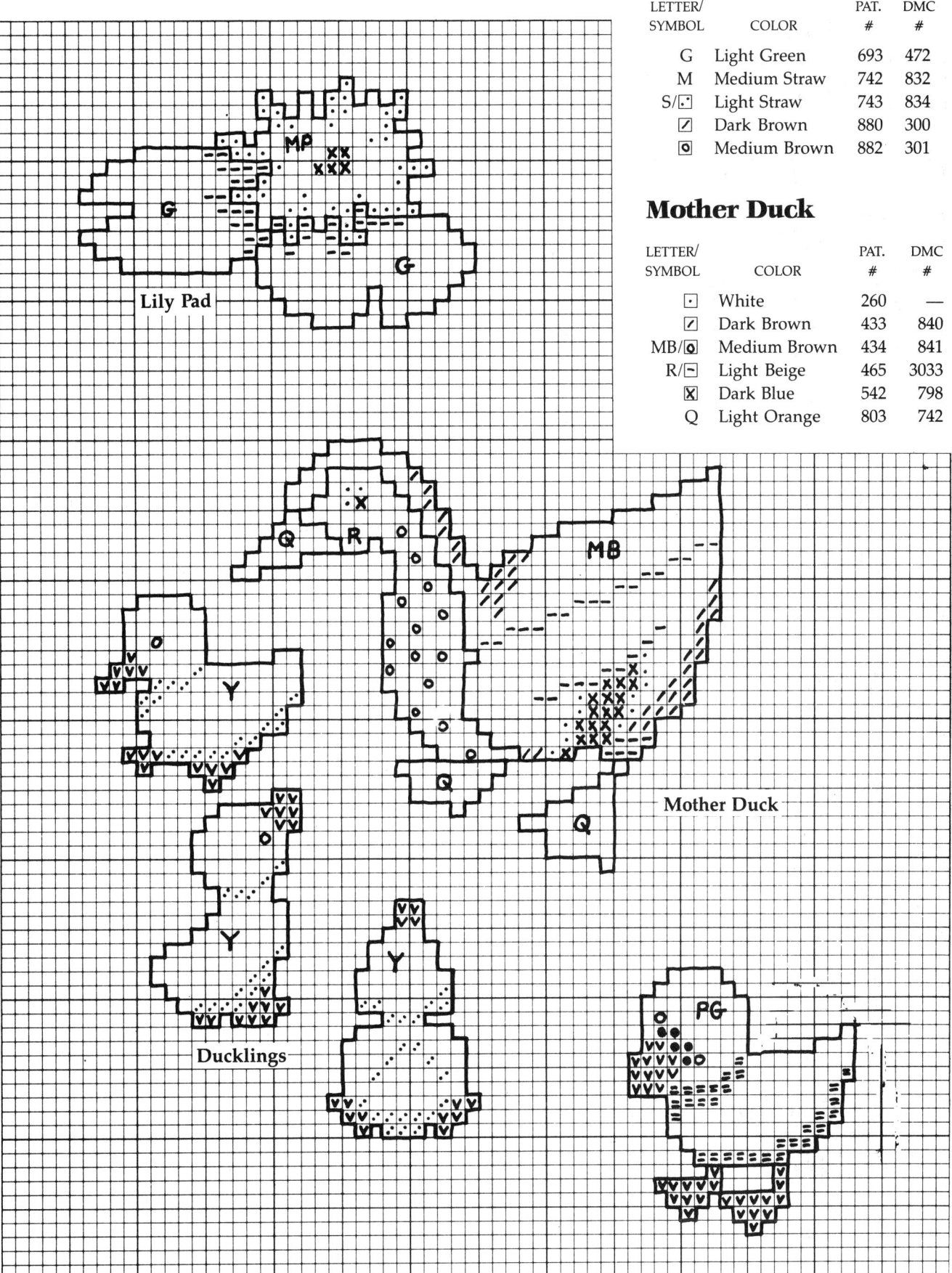

Cattails

LETTER/ SYMBOL	COLOR	PAT. #	DMC #
G	Light Green	693	472
M	Medium Straw	742	832
S/⊡	Light Straw	743	834
☑	Dark Brown	880	300
⊙	Medium Brown	882	301

Mother Duck

LETTER/ SYMBOL	COLOR	PAT. #	DMC #
⊡	White	260	—
☑	Dark Brown	433	840
MB/⊙	Medium Brown	434	841
R/⊟	Light Beige	465	3033
☒	Dark Blue	542	798
Q	Light Orange	803	742

Lily Pad

Mother Duck

Ducklings

The Three Little Pigs

Alternate Top

First Pig

Pigs

LETTER/SYMBOL	COLOR	PAT. #	DMC #	LETTER/SYMBOL	COLOR	PAT. #	DMC #
R/Z	Light Gray	203	648	Y	Yellow	713	726
⊞	Black	220	310	⊘	Dark Brick Red	860	300
W	White	260	—	K	Brick Red	861	301
⁄⁄	Dark Brown	422	801	⊡	Light Brick Red	863	402
⊠	Dark Blue	580	517	S	Dark Rust	880	919
B/⊙	Blue	583	518	⊙	Dark Pink	931	352
⊟	Dark Green	631	701	·	Medium Pink	932	353
G	Green	632	704	P	Light Pink	934	948
☑	Dark Yellow	712	783				

Basket of Apples

LETTER/SYMBOL	COLOR	PAT. #	DMC #	LETTER/SYMBOL	COLOR	PAT. #	DMC #
⊙	Black	220	310	⊡	Yellow	771	742
☑	Dark Straw	741	680	⊠	Dark Red	970	817
M	Medium Straw	742	729	⁄	Red	972	666
L	Light Straw	743	676				

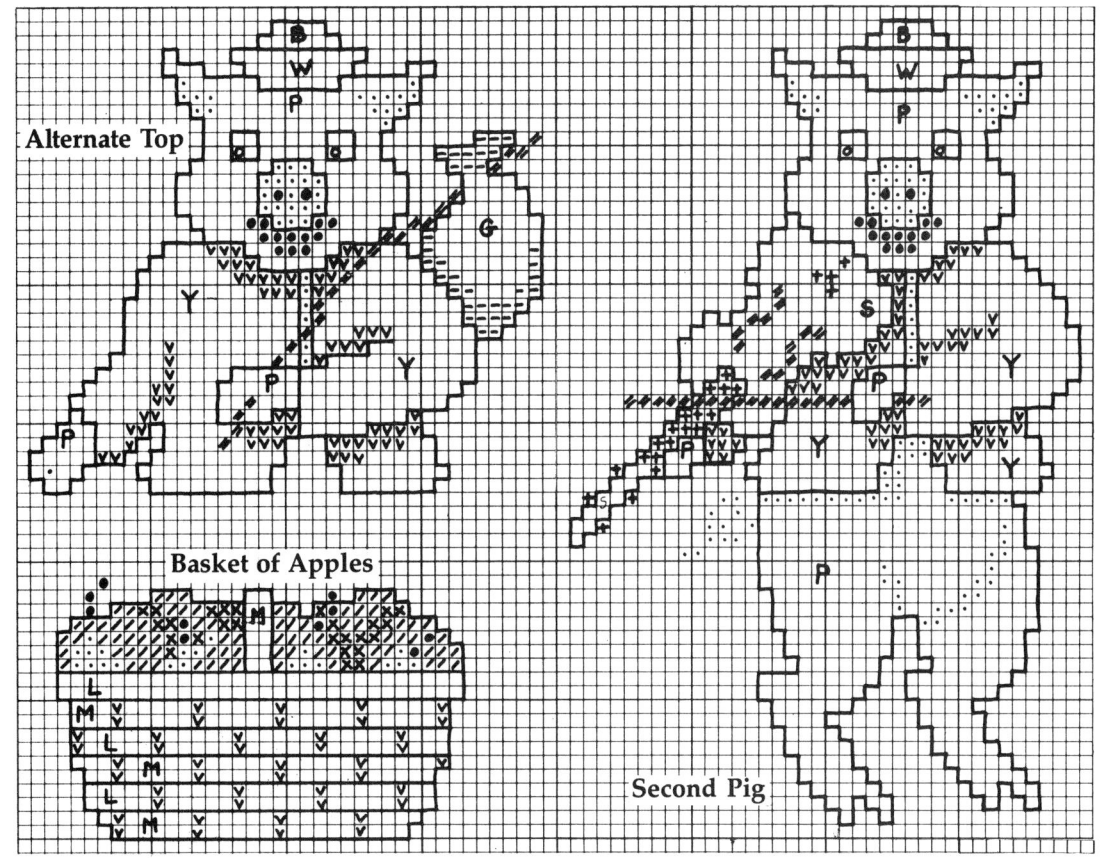

Alternate Top

Basket of Apples

Second Pig

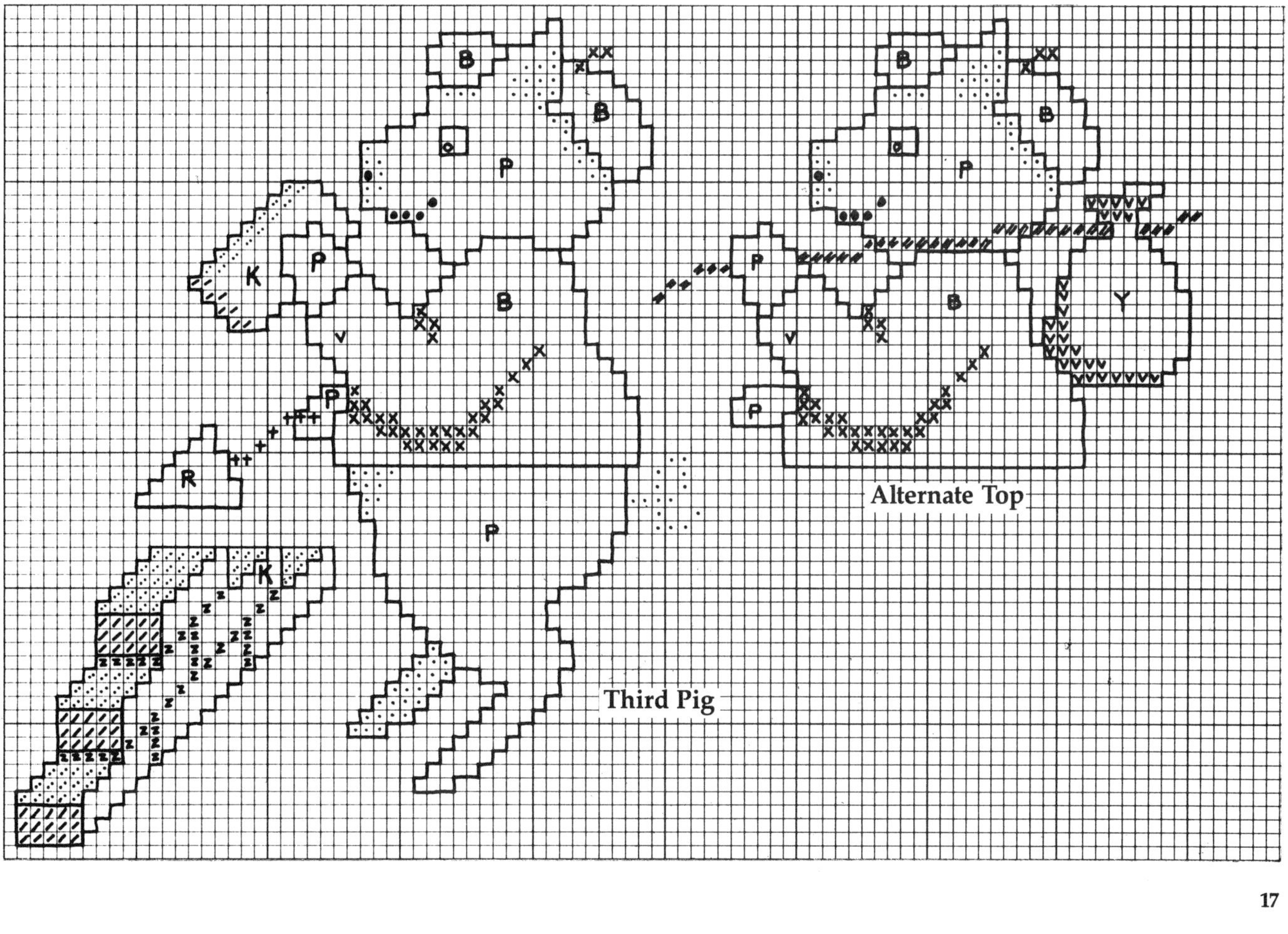

Third Pig

Alternate Top

Cinderella

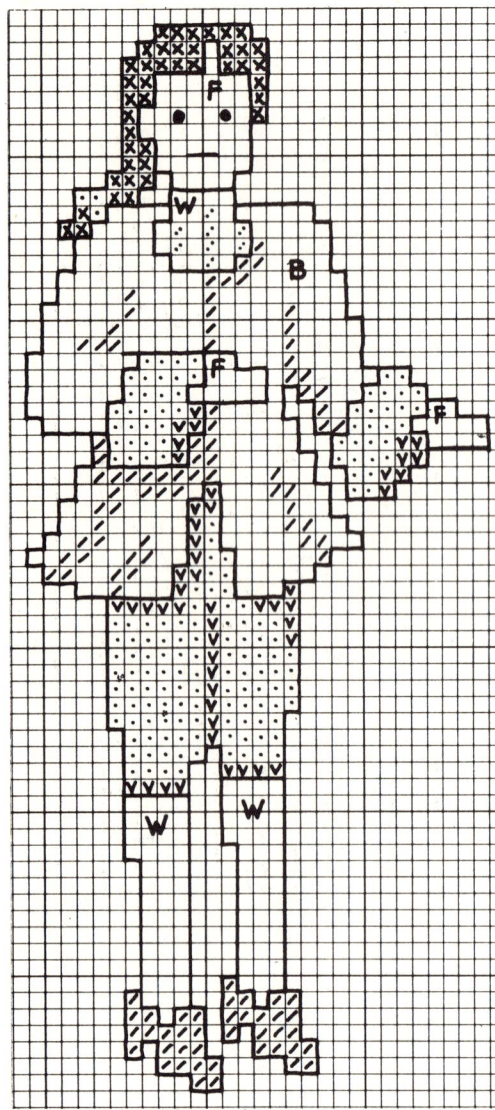

Prince Charming

LETTER/ SYMBOL	COLOR	PAT. #	DMC #
W	White	260	—
⊠	Brown	411	801
F	Flesh	494	712
◪	Dark Blue	582	806
B/◉	Blue	583	807
⬚	Pale Blue	556	747
☑	Dark Gold	712	783
⬚	Gold	713	726
—	*Pink	923	224

*Stitch mouth in straight stitch, over completed stitches.

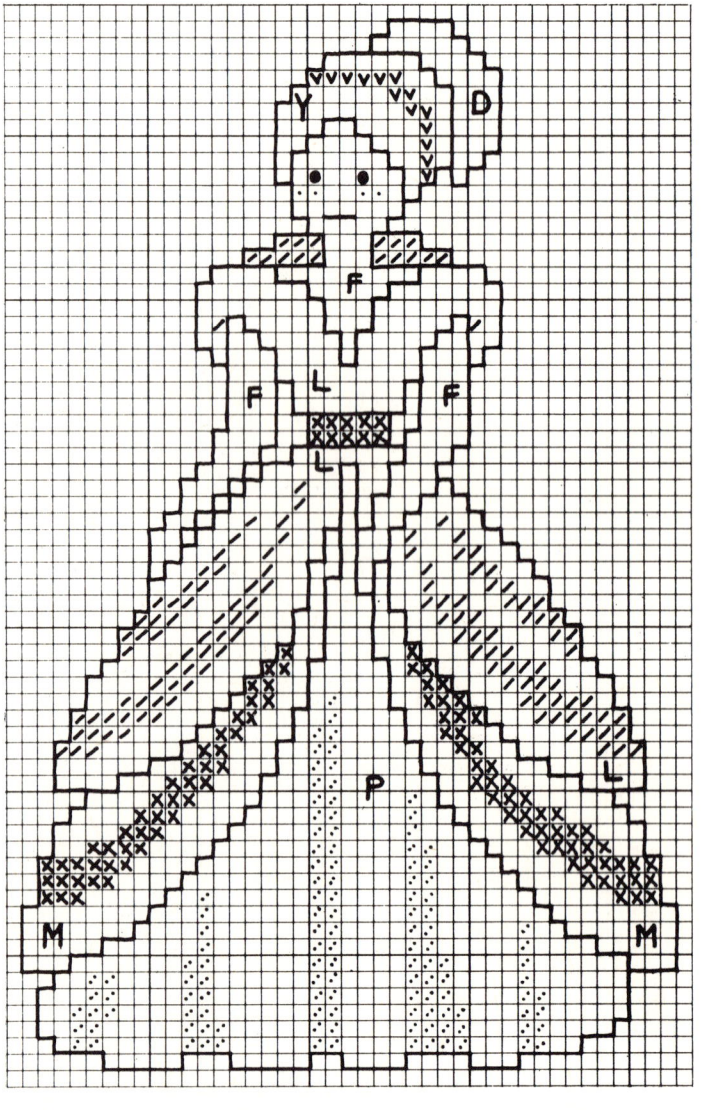

Cinderella

LETTER/ SYMBOL	COLOR	PAT. #	DMC #
◉	Blue	581	517
☑	Dark Gold	743	680
Y	Gold	745	676
D/⊠	Dark Pink	941	326
M/◪	Medium Pink	943	335
L/⬚	*Light Pink	945	3326
P/⬚	Pale Pink	875	818
F	Flesh	948	712

*Stitch mouth in straight stitch, over completed stitches.

Castle

LETTER/ SYMBOL	COLOR	PAT. #	DMC #
D	Dark Gray	200	844
M/☑	Medium Gray	202	646
L	Light Gray	203	648
☒	Black	220	310
B	Light Blue	553	813
Y	Yellow	704	727

Coach

LETTER/ SYMBOL	COLOR	PAT. #	DMC #
▣	*Dark Green	680	909
☒	Medium Green	683	912
M/▭	Light Green	687	955
▣	Dark Gold	712	783
▣	Gold	713	726
Y	Yellow	760	973

*Outline door and wheels in backstitch after all other stitching is complete.

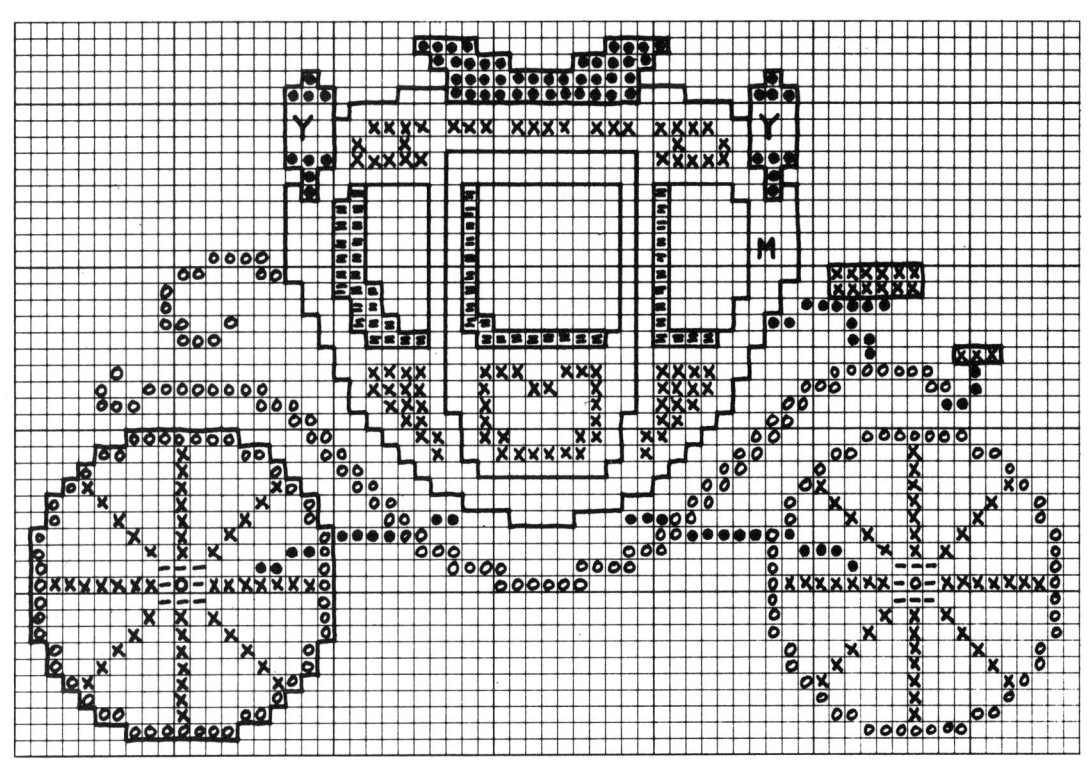

The Hare and the Tortoise

LETTER/ SYMBOL	COLOR	PAT. #	DMC #	LETTER/ SYMBOL	COLOR	PAT. #	DMC #
◉	Charcoal Gray	210	413	⊟	Medium Yellow Green	671	906
PG	Pale Gray	256	762	LY	Light Yellow Green	672	907
W/⊡	White	260	—	ⱽ	Dark Green	692	3345
R	Brown	432	839	G	Medium Green	693	3347
MB	Medium Beige	454	613	LG	Light Green	694	3348
⊟	Dark Blue	550	824	RD/◎	Red	951	349
B/⊠	Medium Blue	552	826	LP/⊞	Light Pink	946	225
LB	Light Blue	556	828				

The Hare and the Tortoise

Hare

LETTER/ SYMBOL	COLOR	PAT. #	DMC #
☑	Medium Gray	202	646
G	Light Gray	203	648
⊡	White	260	—
B	Blue	583	807
⊙	Green	632	704
☒	Yellow	712	973
☑	Pink	933	754

Tortoise

LETTER/ SYMBOL	COLOR	PAT. #	DMC #
⊡	White	260	—
⊙	Blue	552	826
☒	Dark Green	610	895
G	Medium Green	611	3345
☑	Medium Yellow Green	692	470
Q	Light Yellow Green	693	472
D	Dark Gold	732	782

Jack and the Beanstalk

LETTER/ SYMBOL	COLOR	PAT. #	DMC #
⊡	White	260	—
R	Medium Brown	453	611
M	Light Brown	454	612
☑	Dark Blue	551	797
B/⊙	Blue	552	798
☒	Dark Green	631	3345
⊟	Medium Green	632	3346
⊡	Light Green	633	472
Y	Yellow	713	726
☑	Gold	726	783
⊞	Red	841	349
—	*Pink	933	758
⊙	Pale Pink	875	948
F	Flesh	948	712
⊟	Rust	882	976

*Stitch mouth in straight stitch, over completed stitches.

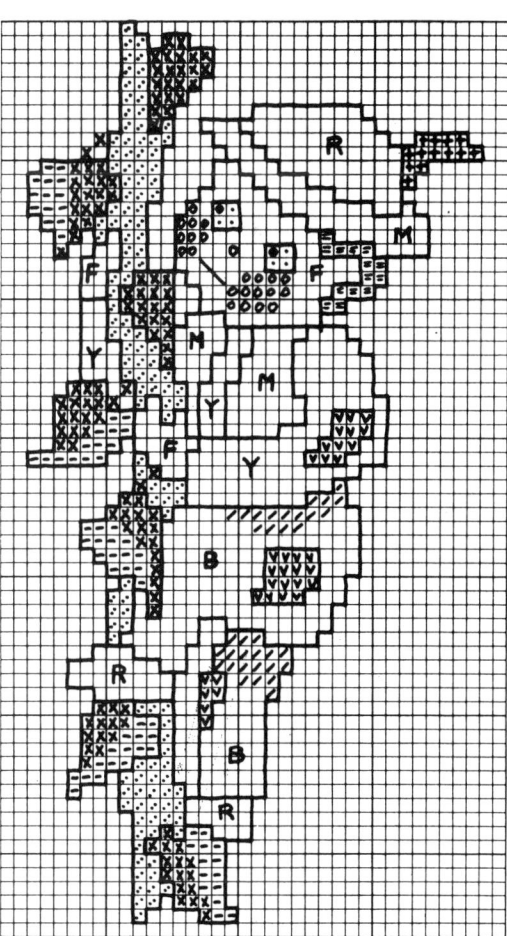

Jack and the Beanstalk

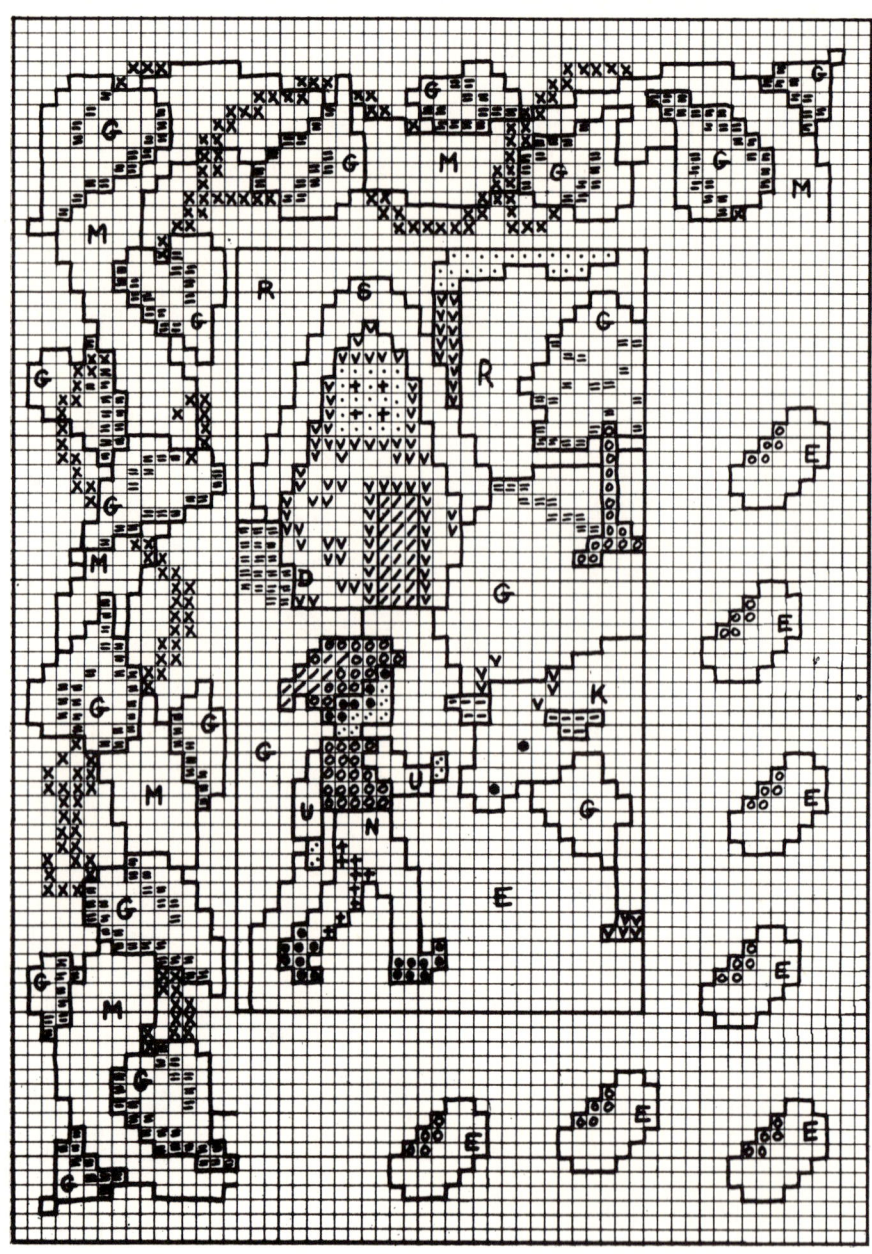

Picture with Two Borders

LETTER/ SYMBOL	COLOR	PAT. #	DMC #	LETTER/ SYMBOL	COLOR	PAT. #	DMC #
Ⓥ	Medium Gray	202	318	R	Pale Blue	556	828
D	Light Gray	203	762	⊟	Dark Green	610	986
⊡	White	260	—	G	Light Green	612	989
⊟	Medium Rust	413	922	⊠	Medium Yellow Green	692	469
K	Light Rust	414	402	M	Pale Yellow Green	694	472
⊙	Dark Brown	431	801	S	Straw	742	834
⊡	Medium Brown	462	841	U	Yellow	773	745
E	Light Beige	475	822	⊡	Flesh	948	712
⊞	Medium Blue	503	826	☑	Red	930	355
N	Light Blue	504	813				

Hansel and Gretel

Gretel

LETTER/ SYMBOL	COLOR	PAT. #	DMC #
W/⊡	White	260	—
B	Brown	424	435
⊠	Blue	543	793
G/✓	Light Green	623	955
⊘	Dark Yellow	712	783
M	Yellow	713	726
⊙	Dark Straw	743	729
Y/⊟	Straw	745	676
⊞	Dark Pink	952	3328
P/ —	*Pink	955	761
⊙	Pale Pink	875	948
F	Pale Flesh	948	712

*Stitch mouth in straight stitch over completed stitches.

Cottage and Border

LETTER/ SYMBOL	COLOR	PAT. #	DMC #
⊡	White	260	—
⊠	Dark Brown	412	433
⊟	Medium Brown	403	436
B	Light Brown	404	738
⊡	Green	684	912
⊘	Yellow	713	727
Y	Light Yellow	714	3078
⊜	Gold	742	680
⊡	Light Gold	743	676
⊙	Red	971	666
⊞	Dark Pink	943	891
P	Light Pink	944	894

Hansel, Birds and Bread Crumbs

LETTER/ SYMBOL	COLOR	PAT. #	DMC #
⊡	White	260	—
⊟	Dark Brown	423	801
N/⊙	Brown	424	435
⊡	Light Brown	443	613
F	Flesh	494	712
⊠	Dark Blue	501	311
⊟	Medium Blue	502	322
B	Light Blue	504	3325
⊡	Blue Green	583	518
S	Light Blue Green	584	519
⊞	Bright Green	633	704
⊘	Yellow	713	725
Y	Light Yellow	714	727
—	*Pink	955	761
⊙	Pale Pink	875	948

The City Mouse and the Country Mouse

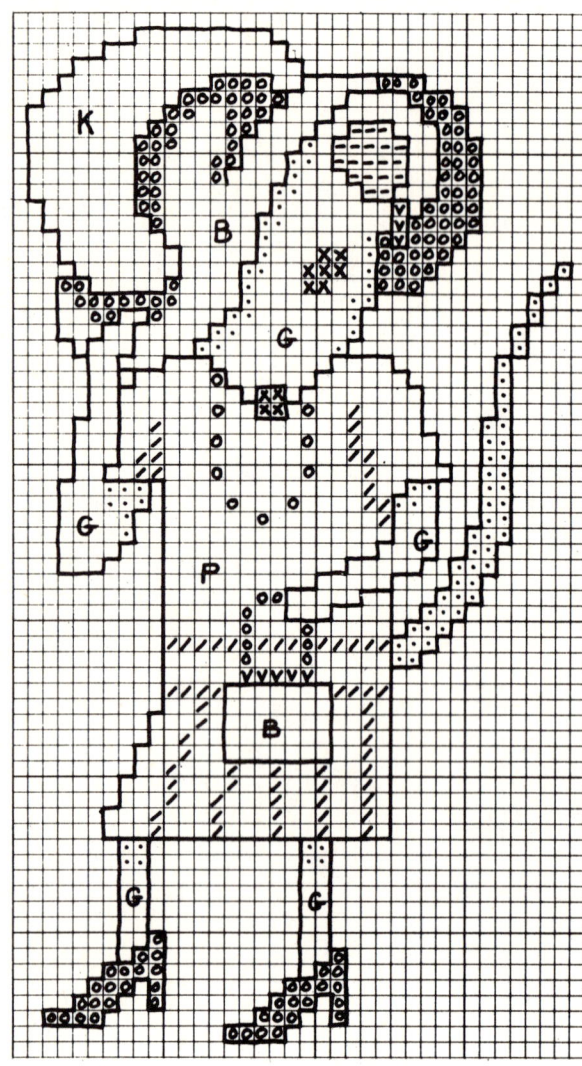

City Mouse

LETTER/ SYMBOL	COLOR	PAT. #	DMC #
⊡	Medium Gray	202	318
G	Light Gray	203	415
☒	Black	220	310
⊙	Dark Green	692	469
B	Medium Green	693	471
☑	Yellow	771	742
K/☑	Pink	943	899
P	Light Pink	945	776
⊟	Light Rusty Pink	934	761

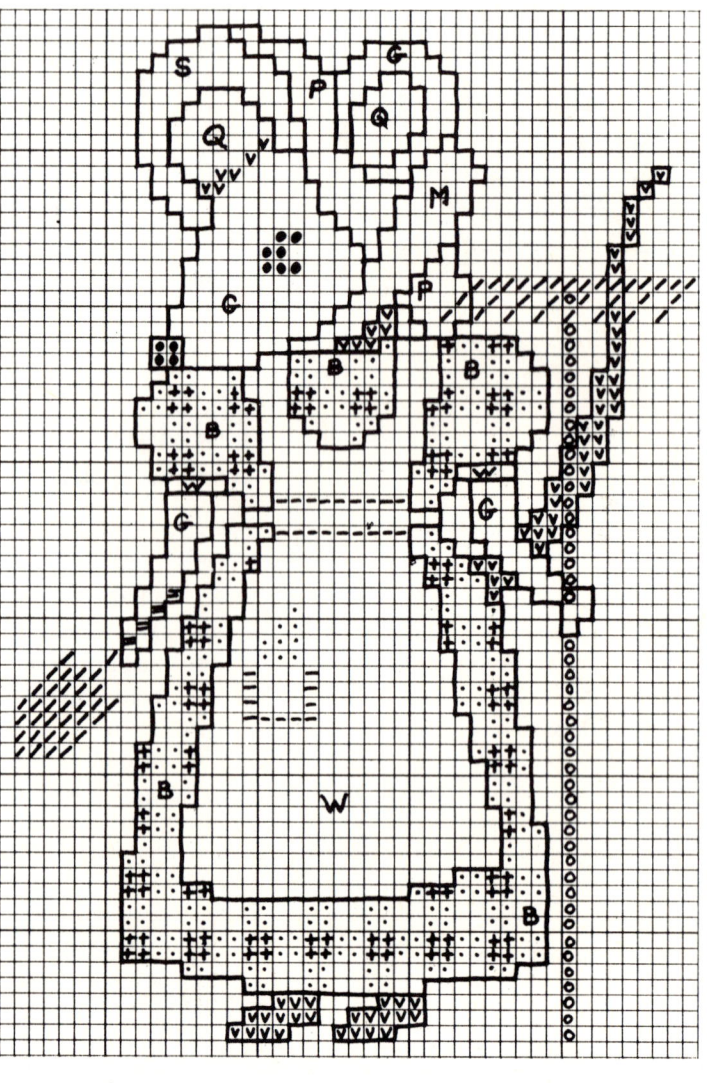

Country Mouse

LETTER/ SYMBOL	COLOR	PAT. #	DMC #
☑	Charcoal Gray	221	844
☑	Medium Gray	202	452
G	Light Gray	203	453
⊙	Black	220	310
W	White	260	—
⊞	Dark Blue	550	824
⊡	Medium Blue	552	826
B/⊟	Light Blue	554	827
S	Dark Straw	742	680
P/⊙	Straw	745	676
⊟	Red	941	304
M	Pink	943	899
Q	Light Rusty Pink	934	761

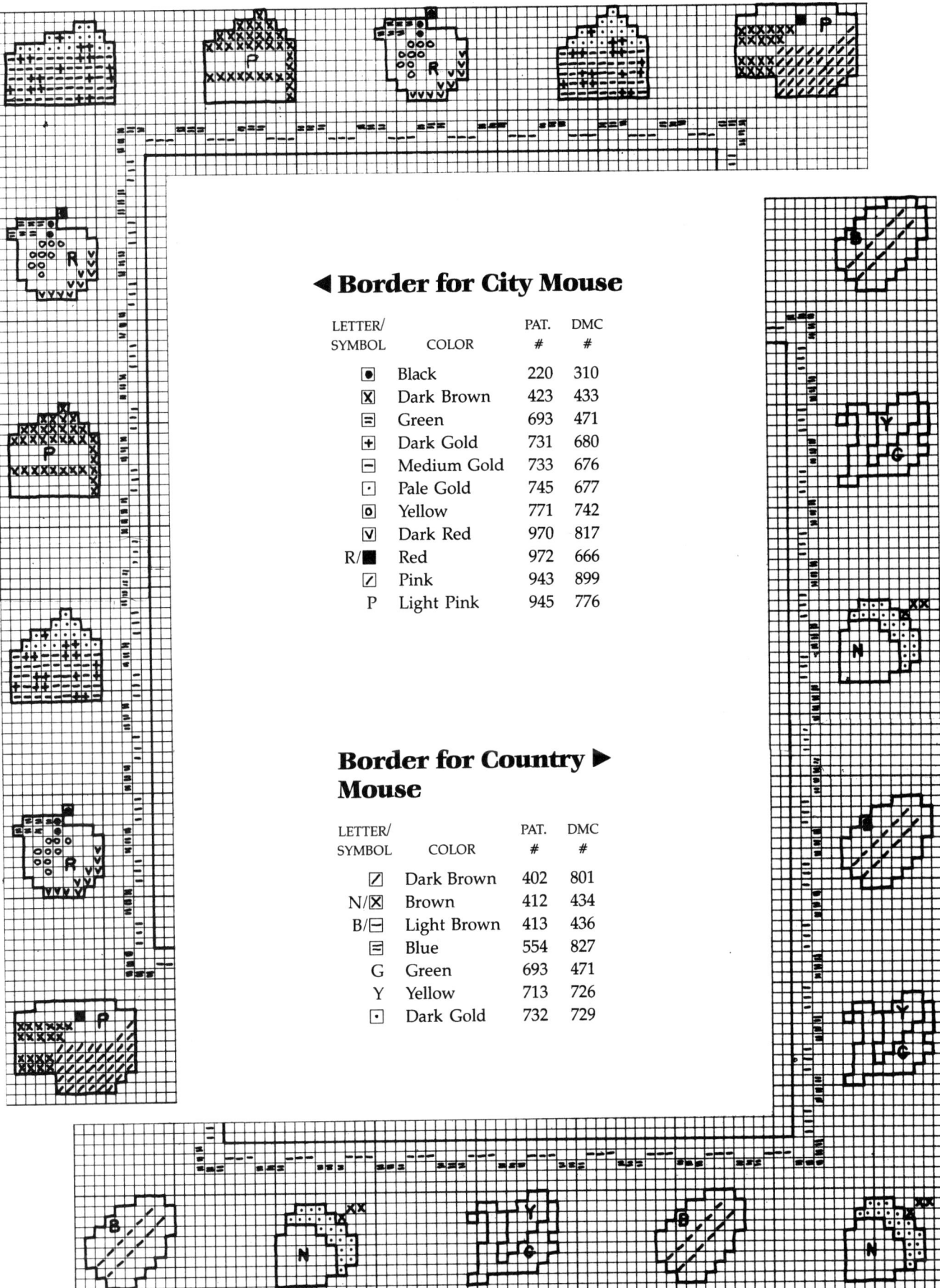

◀ Border for City Mouse

LETTER/ SYMBOL	COLOR	PAT. #	DMC #
⊙	Black	220	310
☒	Dark Brown	423	433
⊟	Green	693	471
⊞	Dark Gold	731	680
⊟	Medium Gold	733	676
⊡	Pale Gold	745	677
⊙	Yellow	771	742
V	Dark Red	970	817
R/■	Red	972	666
⊿	Pink	943	899
P	Light Pink	945	776

Border for Country ▶ Mouse

LETTER/ SYMBOL	COLOR	PAT. #	DMC #
⊿	Dark Brown	402	801
N/☒	Brown	412	434
B/⊟	Light Brown	413	436
⊟	Blue	554	827
G	Green	693	471
Y	Yellow	713	726
⊡	Dark Gold	732	729

The Gingerbread Boy

LETTER/ SYMBOL	COLOR	PAT. #	DMC #
⊟	Dark Gray	200	646
☑	Light Gray	203	648
◉	Black	220	310
W/⊡	White	260	—
☒	Dark Brown	411	898
G	Gingerbread	412	436
Y/⊟	Yellow	714	3078
⊘	Dark Rust	880	919
S	Rust	883	921
R	Red	841	666
⊙	Dark Pink	953	3328
⊞	Light Pink	934	761

Cinderella
Color Chart

stepsisters	stepmother	Cinderella	mouse	mop	pail	pumpkin	plant	lantern	chandelier	candle/holder	sconces	perfume shelf	perfumes	stool	mirror/table	drapes	window lead	windows	door	woodwork	carpet	floor	hearth	stones	walls	roof windows	stucco/trim	shingles	No.	Color	Group
					×			×											×									×	220	BLACK	GRAY
	×	×							×	×														×				×	221	Charcoal	GRAY
																								×	×				200	Dk.	GRAY
		×	×															×						×	×				202	Med.	GRAY
					×																				×				203	Lt.	GRAY
					×																								204	Pale	GRAY
		×										×						×		×									260	WHITE	
		×																											312	Med. Grape	PURPLE
																×													321	Dk. Plum	PURPLE
											×				×	×				×					×				322	Med. Plum	PURPLE
																				×					×				324	Lt. Plum	PURPLE
																									×				325	Pale Plum	PURPLE
			×																										402	Dk. Fawn	BROWN
			×																										403	Med. Fawn	BROWN
																						×	×						405	Lt. Fawn	BROWN
																										×			406	Pale Fawn	BROWN
×																				×	×							×	411	Dk. Earth Brown	BROWN
																				×	×								424	Med. Coffee Brown	BROWN
×									×																				883	Med. Ginger	BROWN
									×																				884	Lt. Ginger	BROWN
																×													236	Pale Blue Gray	BLUE
		×																											541	Dk. Cobalt	BLUE
		×																											543	Med. Cobalt	BLUE
			×																										581	Dk. Sky Blue	BLUE
			×																										583	Med. Sky Blue	BLUE
			×									×																	585	Lt. Sky Blue	BLUE
								×	×																				631	Dk. Green	GREEN
×		×																			×								633	Med. Green	GREEN
×																													634	Lt. Green	GREEN
												×																	701	Med. Butterscotch	YELLOW/ORANGE
		×										×	×	×	×	×													702	Lt. Butterscotch	YELLOW/ORANGE
																										×			713	Med. Mustard	YELLOW/ORANGE
																		×							×				714	Lt. Mustard	YELLOW/ORANGE
																					×								715	Pale Mustard	YELLOW/ORANGE
																									×				754	Dk. Gold	YELLOW/ORANGE
																									×				755	Med. Gold	YELLOW/ORANGE
																									×				756	Lt. Gold	YELLOW/ORANGE
		×						×			×								×										772	Yellow	YELLOW/ORANGE
										×																			843	Dk. Orange	YELLOW/ORANGE
										×									×										802	Med. Orange	YELLOW/ORANGE
											×								×										804	Lt. Orange	YELLOW/ORANGE
				×				×																					841	Red	RED/PINK
	×	×																											875	Pale Rust	RED/PINK
×		×												×															943	Dk. Pink	RED/PINK
×														×							×								944	Med. Pink	RED/PINK
×																					×								945	Lt. Pink	RED/PINK
×																													946	Pale Pink	RED/PINK

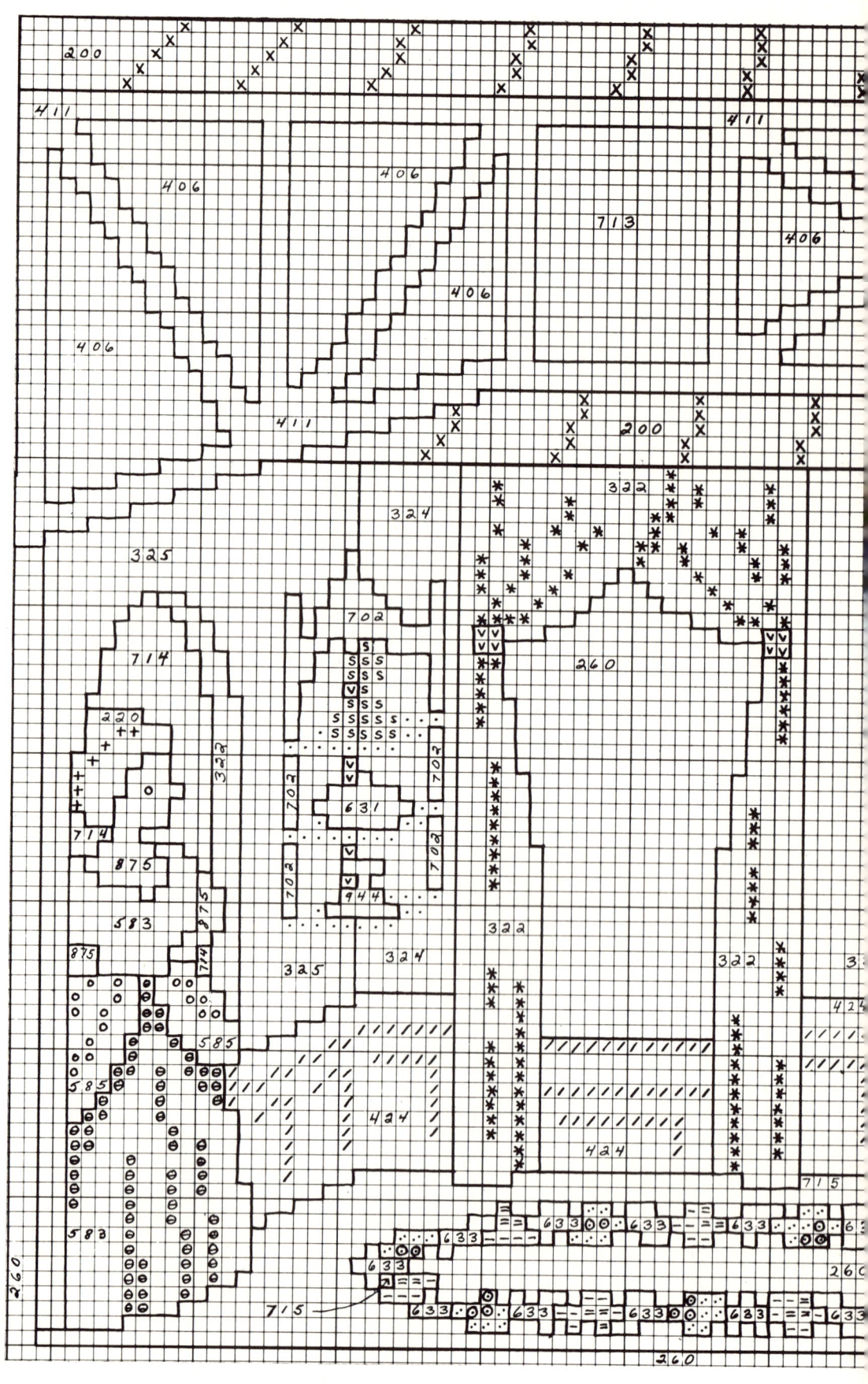

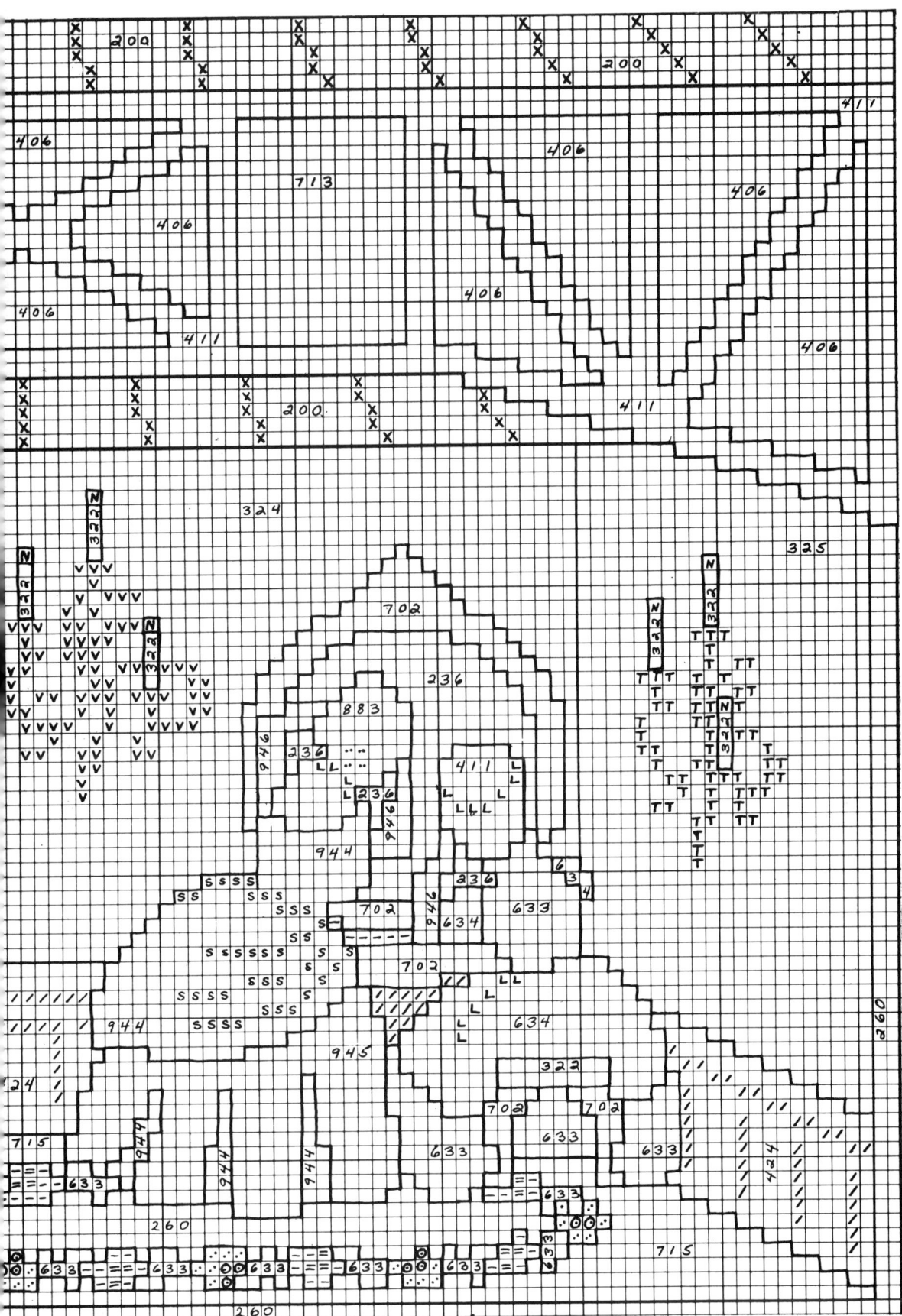

See color chart on page 27 and color key on pages 30–31.

Cinderella—*Downstairs*

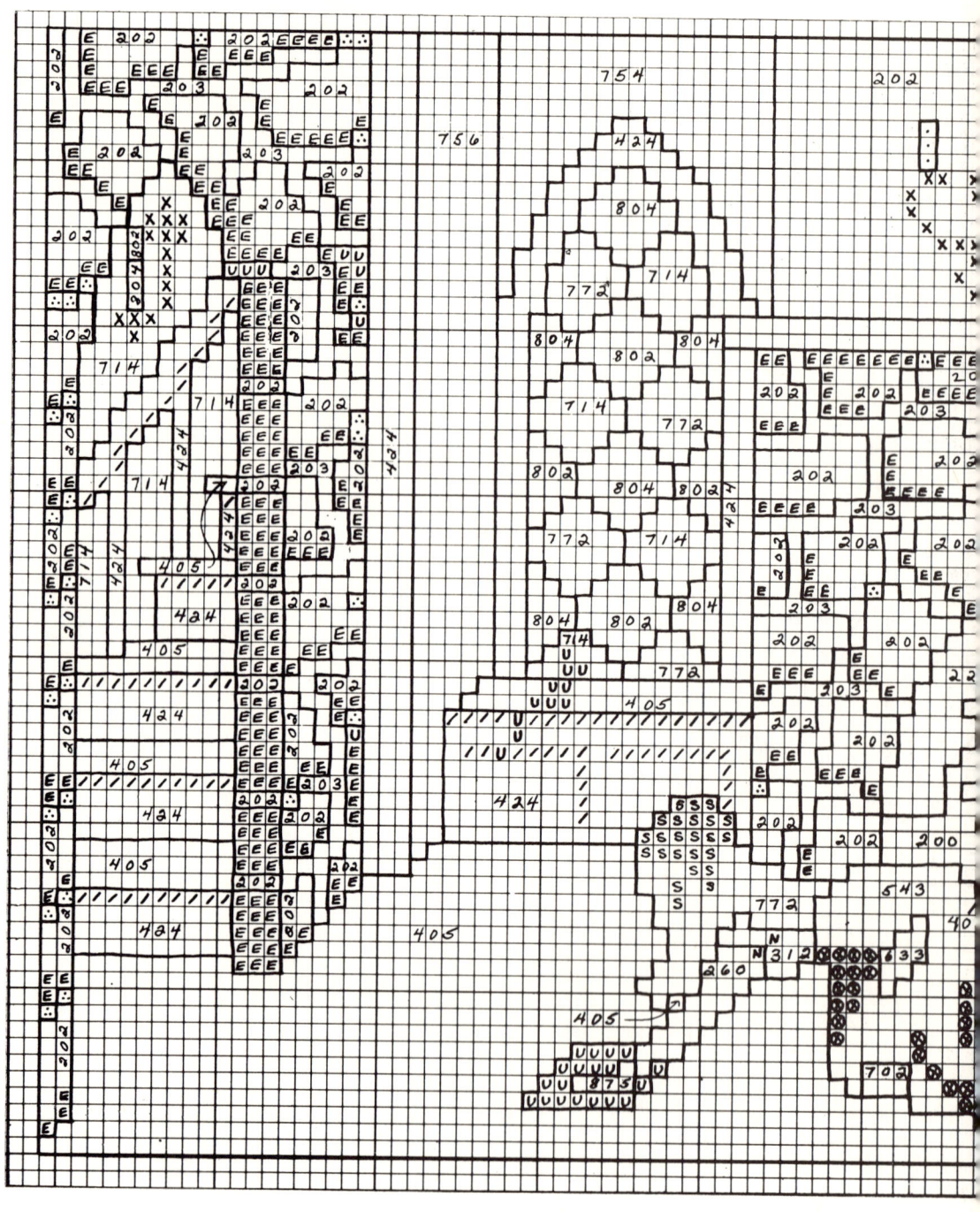

SYMBOL	PAT. #	COLOR
●	220	Black
X	221	Charcoal Gray
E	200	Dark Gray
U	202	Medium Gray
∴	203	Light Gray
·	260	White

SYMBOL	PAT. #	COLOR
✱	321	Dark Plum
≡	322	Medium Plum
−	324	Light Plum
∕	411	Dark Earth Brown
Z	424	Medium Coffee Brown
⊗	541	Dark Cobalt Blue

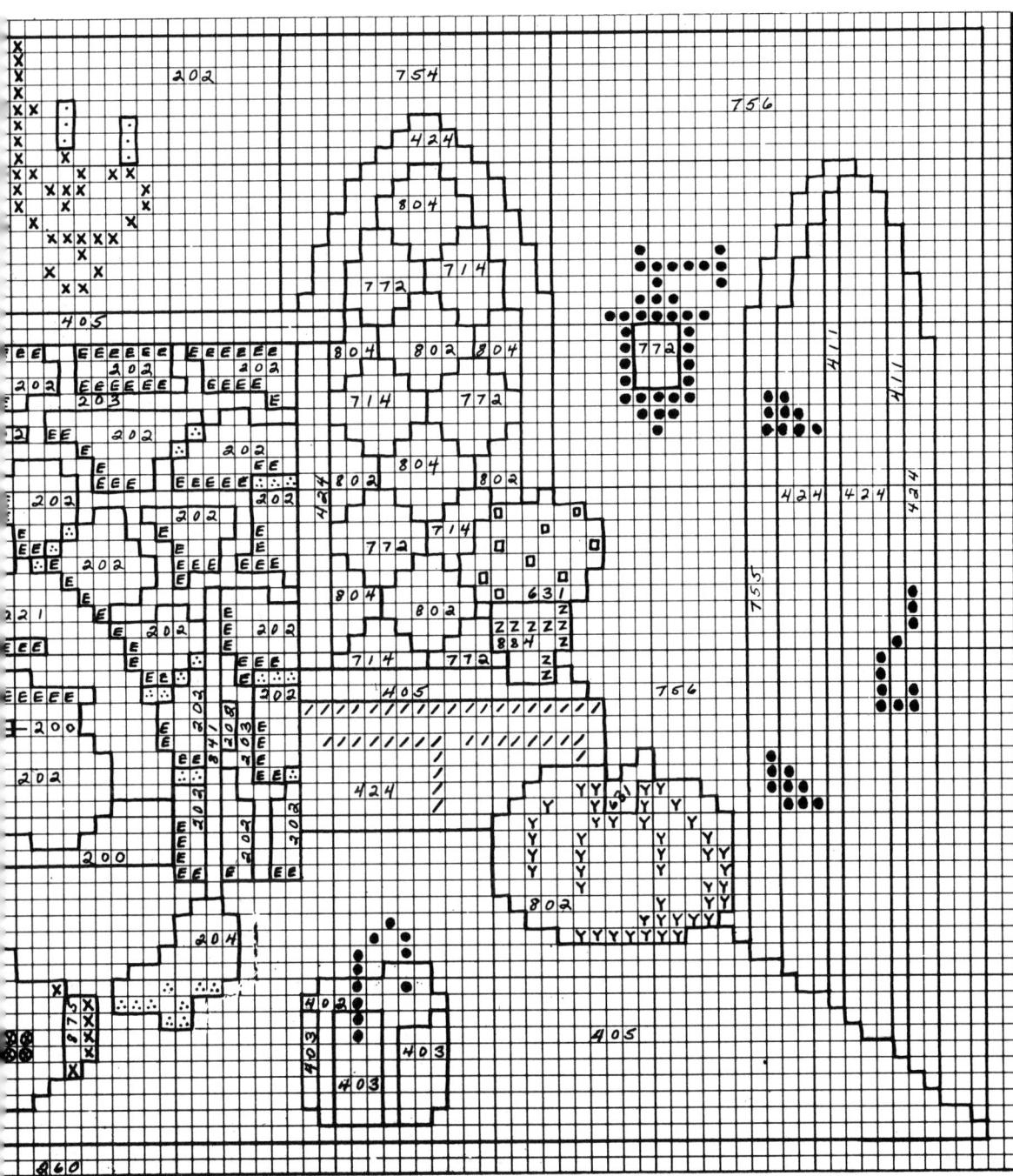

See color chart on page 27.

SYMBOL	PAT. #	COLOR
Ө	581	Dark Sky Blue
O	583	Medium Sky Blue
+	585	Light Blue
L	633	Medium Green
T	701	Medium Butterscotch Yellow
V	702	Light Butterscotch Yellow

SYMBOL	PAT. #	COLOR
N	772	Yellow
Y	843	Dark Orange
☐	841	Red
S	943	Dark Pink
O	944	Medium Pink
··	945	Light Pink

Over-Stitched Details for Cinderella

Work all over-stitching with a single strand of yarn, after all other stitching has been completed and piece has been blocked.

Work window leading in straight stitch with 202 Medium Gray.

Upstairs window

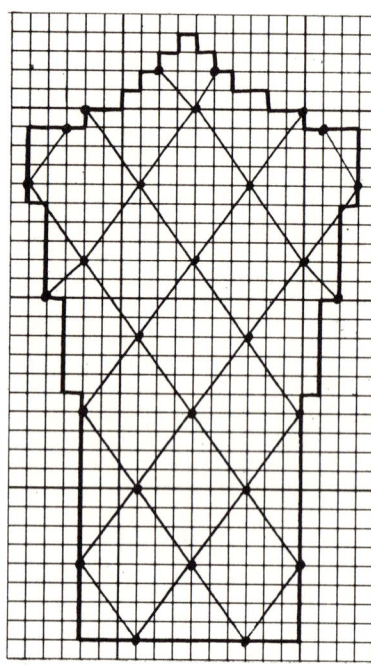

Downstairs windows

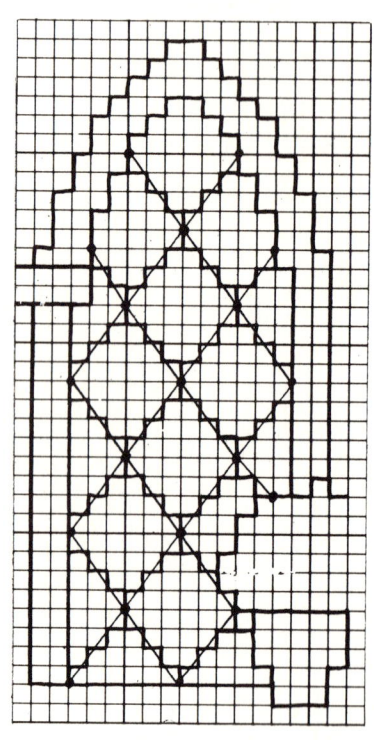

Roof windows

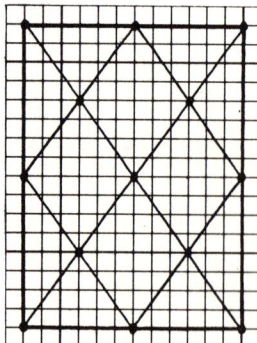

Stepsister's hair

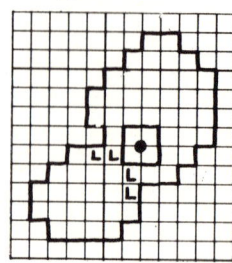

Work French knot with 943 Dark Pink.

Goldilocks and the Three Bears
Color Chart

	GRAY				BROWN							BLUE								GREEN				YELLOW									FLESH	RED			
	220 BLACK	210 Dk.	202 Med.	260 WHITE	402 Dk. Fawn	403 Med. Fawn	406 Pale Fawn	412 Dk. Earth Brown	413 Med. Earth Brown	414 Lt. Earth Brown	870 Dk. Rust	542 Dk. Cobalt	544 Med. Cobalt	545 Lt. Cobalt	554 Lt. Ice Blue	556 Pale Ice Blue	581 Dk. Sky Blue	583 Med. Sky Blue	584 Lt. Sky Blue	631 Dk. Green	632 Med. Green	633 Lt. Green	634 Pale Green	702 Med. Butterscotch	703 Lt. Butterscotch	713 Med. Mustard	714 Lt. Mustard	751 Dk. Gold	752 Med. Gold	754 Lt. Gold	770 Dk. Yellow	772 Lt. Yellow	875 FLESH	941 Red	943 Dk. Pink	944 Med. Pink	945 Lt. Pink
roof shingles																												×	×								
dormer			×		×		×																														
walls												×	×	×								×	×			×	×										
window/door frames			×									×								×				×													
window leading			×																																		
sky																		×																			
carpet																							×														
floor										×																											
floor tiles				×										×																							
beds					×	×											×	×																	×	×	
bedspreads			×												×	×							×	×	×										×		
shelves												×								×																	
train	×													×							×										×			×			
books & pipe	×										×							×			×										×	×		×			
boat & blocks			×	×								×	×																						×		
hats					×	×						×																		×				×		×	
yarn/basket/needles													×			×													×			×					
bedroom lamp																											×					×					
living room lamp			×																												×	×					
flowers & vase												×									×	×				×									×		×
living room table																					×																
door	×	×																																	×	×	
living room chairs																				×	×	×						×	×					×		×	×
kitchen chairs																																			×		
stove	×	×		×																									×		×	×		×			
teakettle	×		×																															×			
tablecloth																						×	×														
fern																				×	×	×	×			×											
bowls																																			×		
candle	×																																		×		
tree branch									×											×																	
bird/house	×																	×	×																×		×
Baby Bear								×	×			×	×																						×		
Mama Bear	×	×		×				×	×	×		×																							×		
Papa Bear	×	×		×				×	×	×	×									×																	
Goldilocks	×			×																															×	×	

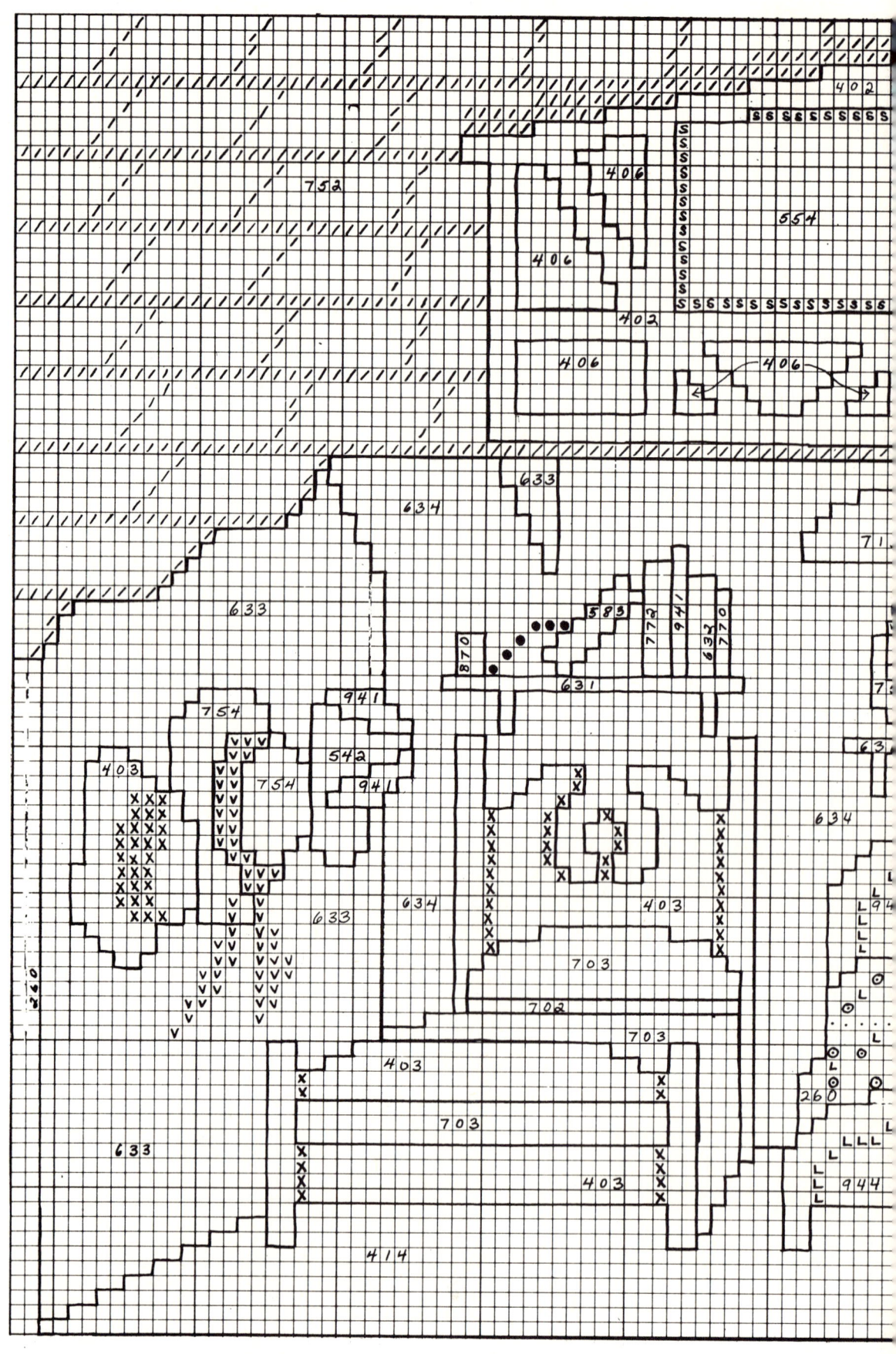

See color chart on page 33 and color key on pages 36–37.

Goldilocks and the Three Bears—*Downstairs*

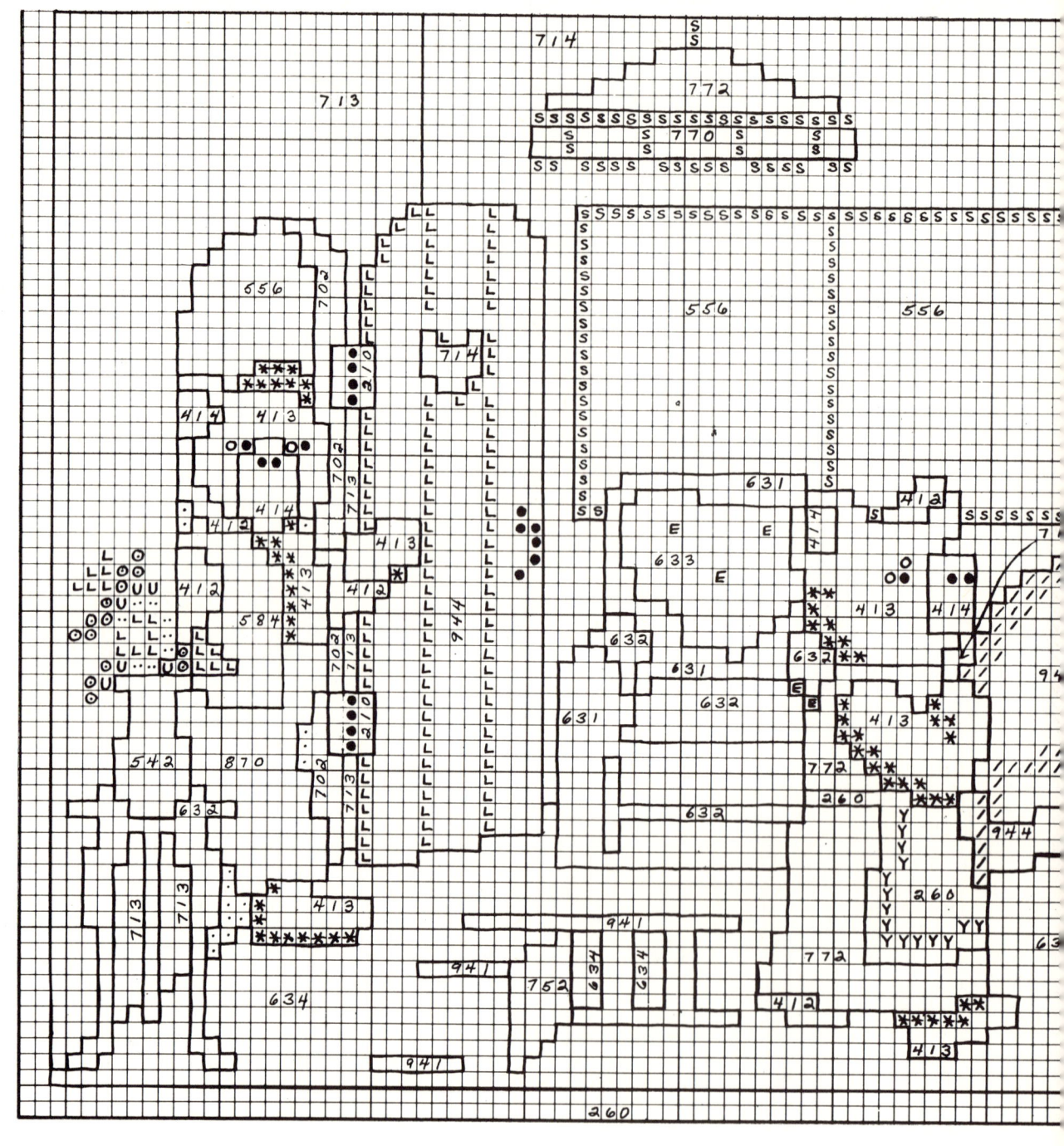

SYMBOL	PAT. #	COLOR		SYMBOL	PAT. #	COLOR
S	202	Medium Gray		N	413	Medium Earth Brown
•	220	Black		Y	542	Dark Cobalt Blue
O	260	White		·	556	Pale Ice Blue
X	402	Dark Fawn Brown		T	581	Dark Sky Blue
✱	412	Dark Earth Brown		+	583	Medium Sky Blue

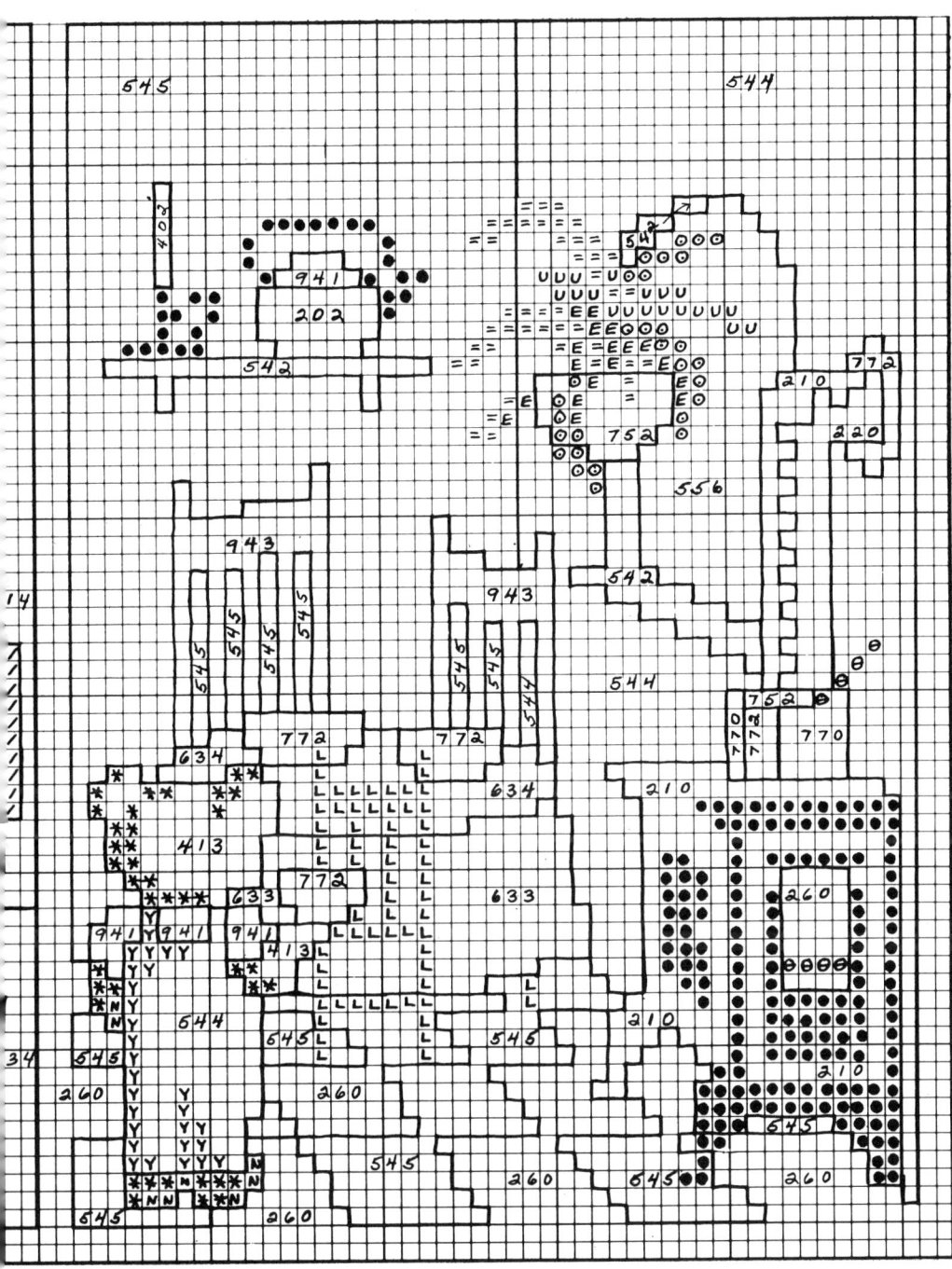

See color chart on page 33.

SYMBOL	PAT. #	COLOR
—	584	Light Sky Blue
E	631	Dark Green
U	632	Medium Green
O	633	Light Green
∕	751	Dark Gold

SYMBOL	PAT. #	COLOR
O	941	Red
L	943	Dark Pink
V	944	Medium Pink
··	945	Light Pink

Over-Stitched Details for Goldilocks and the Three Bears

Work all over-stitching in straight stitch with a single strand of the color indicated, after all other stitching has been completed and piece has been blocked.

Work window leading with 202 Medium Gray.

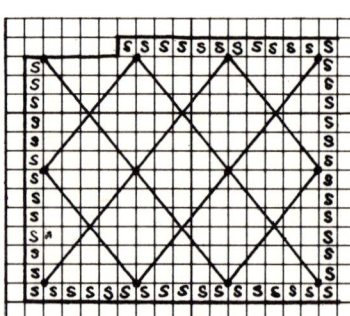

Upstairs window

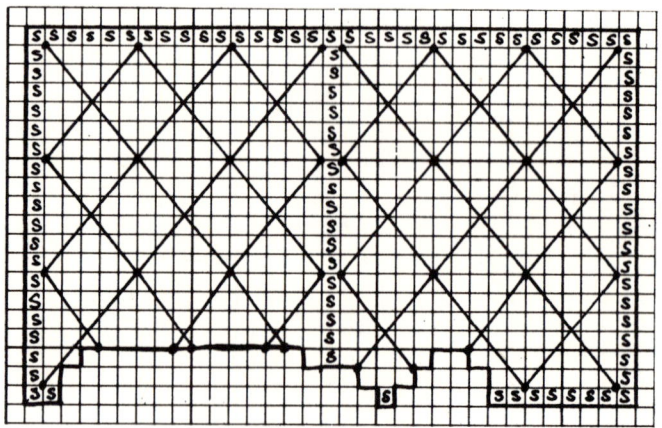

Downstairs window

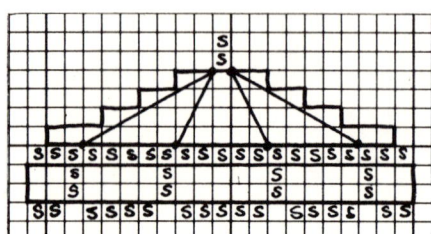

Hanging lamp, downstairs
202 Medium Gray

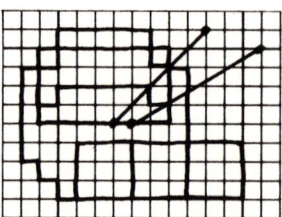

Knitting needles, upstairs at center
770 Dark Sunny Yellow

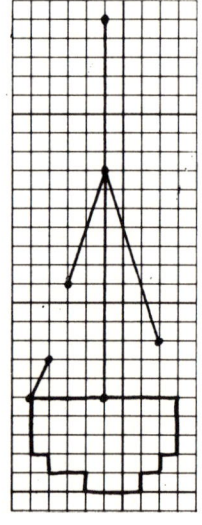

Hanging basket, downstairs
752 Medium Gold

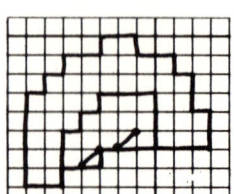

Goldilocks' eyes
220 Black

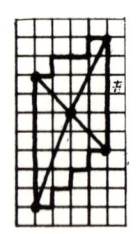

Seat of red chair,
downstairs at left
752 Medium Gold

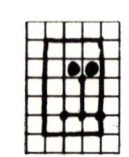

Mama Bear's nose
210 Dark Gray

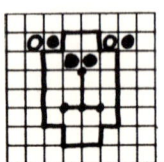

Papa Bear's nose
210 Dark Gray

Little Red Riding Hood
Color Chart

	210	220	260	332	401	404	405	871	873	546	581	583	584	621	622	623	631	633	701	703	751	753	760	812	875	940	941	943	944	945	946
					BROWN					**BLUE**				**GREEN**					**YELLOW**							**RED/PINK**					
	CHARCOAL GRAY	BLACK	WHITE	PURPLE	Dk. Brown	Lt. Brown	Pale Brown	Dk. Rust	Lt. Rust	Pale Cobalt	Dk. Sky Blue	Med. Sky Blue	Lt. Sky Blue	Med. Shamrock Green	Lt. Shamrock Green	Pale Shamrock Green	Dk. Spring	Med. Spring	Dk. Butterscotch	Lt. Butterscotch	Dk. Gold	Med. Gold	Lt. Daffodil Yellow	ORANGE	FLESH	Dk. Red	Red	Dk. Pink	Med. Pink	Lt. Pink	Pale Pink
shingles											×	×																			
shutters																										×	×				
roof windowpanes											×																				
dormers/windows/curtains			×							×																			×		
sky												×																			
walls/shading														×	×	×														×	×
floors							×																								
closet/chairs/table	×																											×	×		
oval rug			×							×							×											×			
square rug																			×				×								
bed			×											×			×		×	×											
globe lamp			×							×				×							×	×				×		×			
oil lamp/shelf		×	×					×											×												
hanging lamp			×																	×											
washstand/spice cabinet			×					×	×																						
round tablecloth											×	×																			
square tablecloth			×							×				×												×			×		
plant/table													×				×	×	×			×									
picture		×	×																												
basket												×									×	×									
towel/bar			×		×							×																			
canisters/shelf			×		×																								×		
bird & branch	×																×					×							×	×	
door		×	×																×			×									
stove	×	×																				×									
saucepan		×																				×									
kettle		×						×	×													×									
iron/shelf		×			×																×										
coffee grinder/stool		×									×	×									×	×									
cup & jar																		×				×						×			
scale		×																	×												
bed warmer		×											×						×	×											
fruit/bowl				×										×								×				×	×		×		
pitcher/bowl & plate			×							×																					
tree																		×													
wolf		×	×		×	×				×																					
Red Riding Hood		×	×														×					×				×	×	×			
Grandma			×							×	×	×	×													×				×	
cat	×		×															×												×	

39

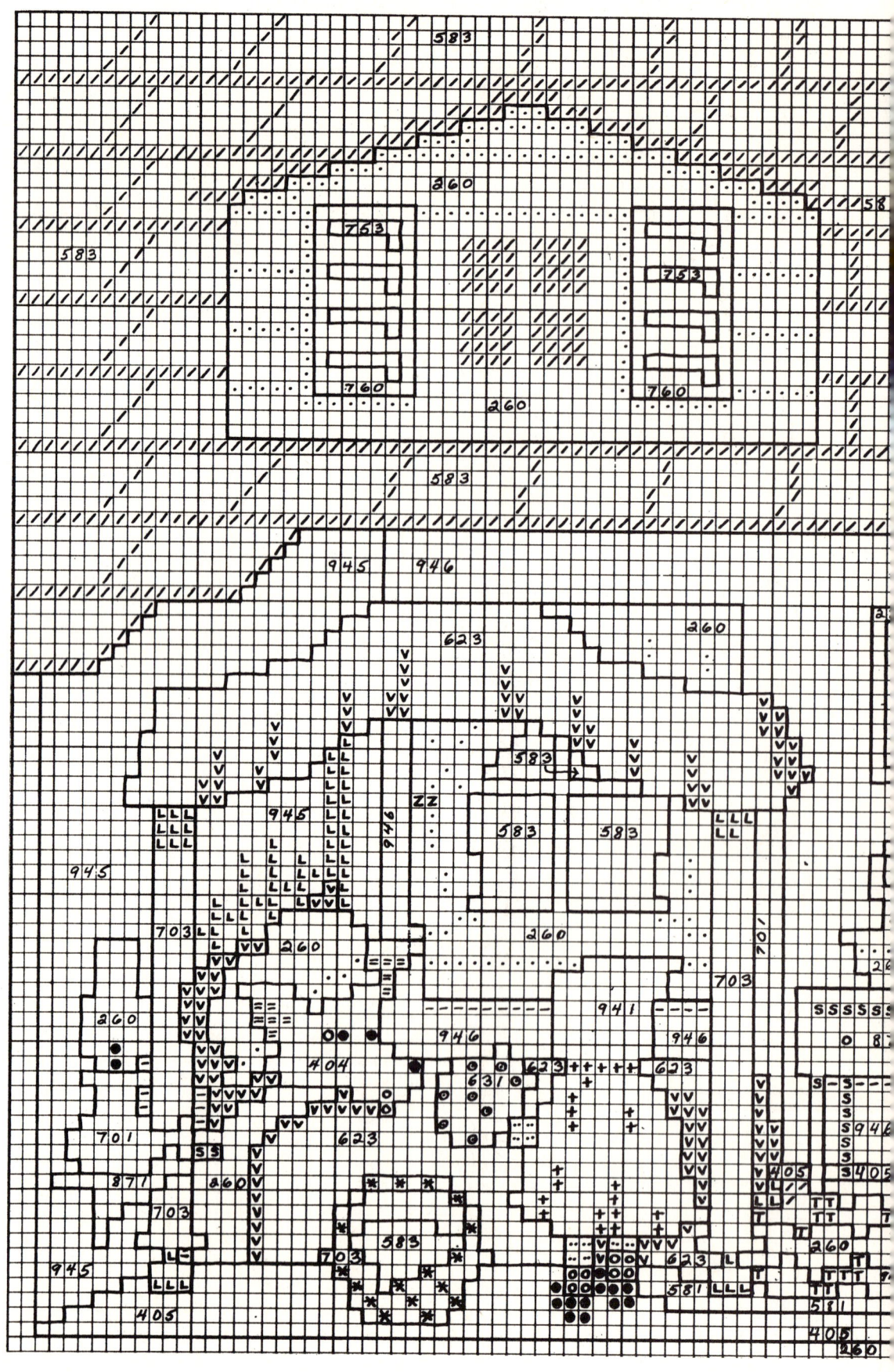

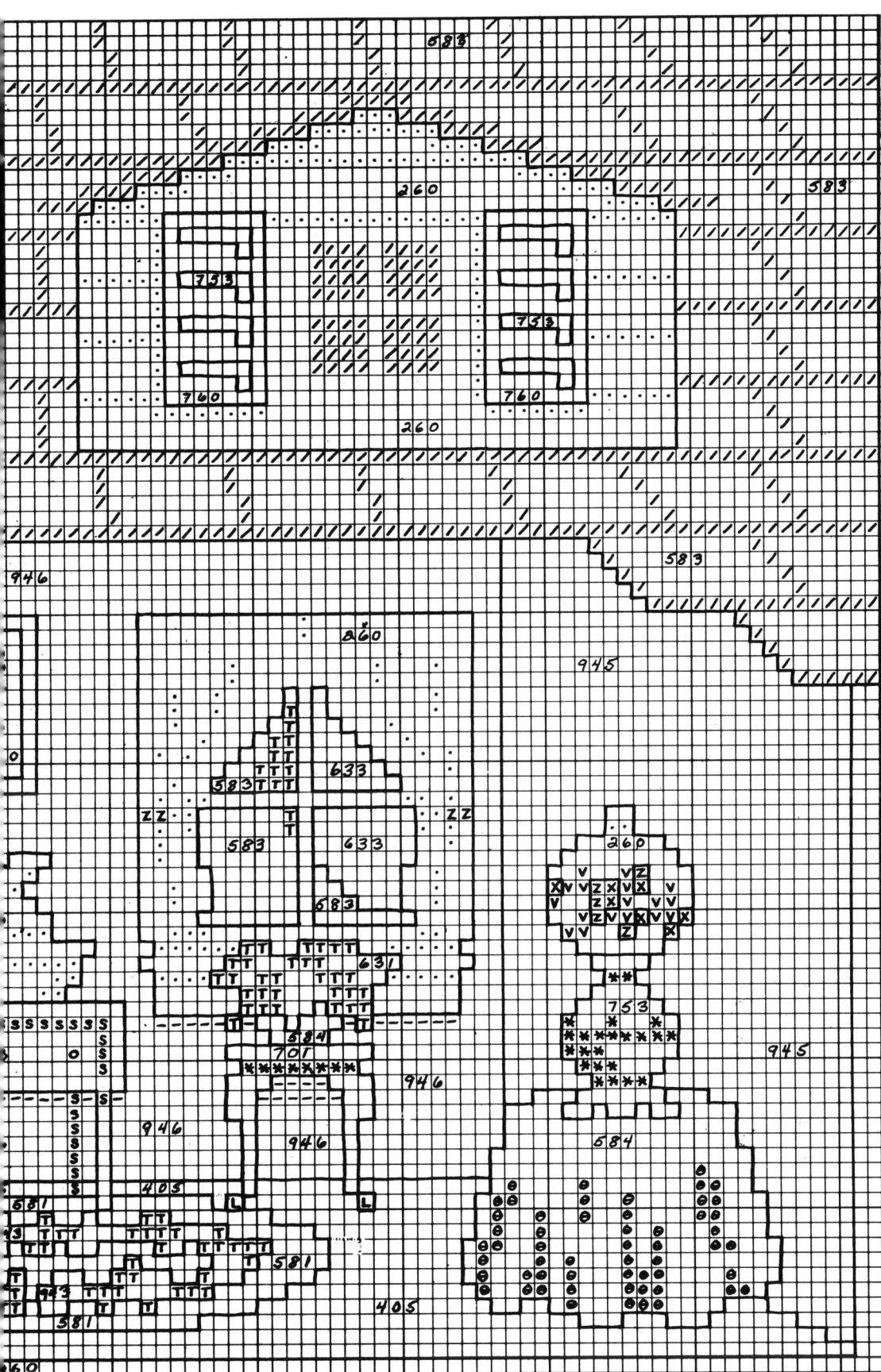

See color chart on page 39 and color key on pages 42–43.

Little Red Riding Hood—*Downstairs*

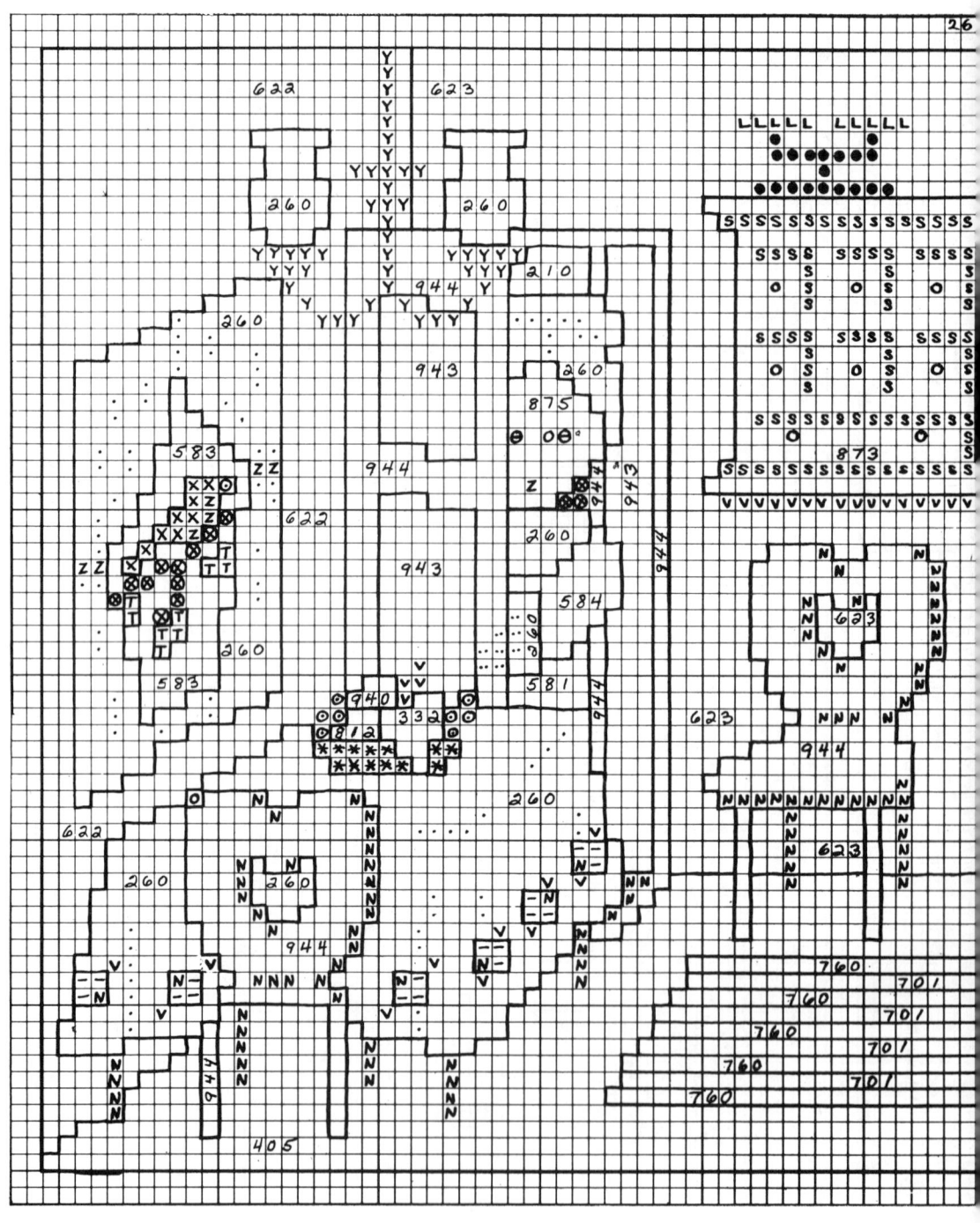

SYMBOL	PAT. #	COLOR		SYMBOL	PAT. #	COLOR
⊗	210	Charcoal Gray		⊖	583	Medium Sky Blue
●	220	Black		V	621	Medium Shamrock Green
○	260	White		U	622	Light Shamrock Green
=	401	Dark Brown		T	633	Medium Spring Green
S	871	Dark Rust		L	701	Dark Butterscotch Yellow
·	546	Pale Cobalt Blue		Y	703	Light Butterscotch Yellow
╱	581	Dark Sky Blue		✻	751	Dark Gold

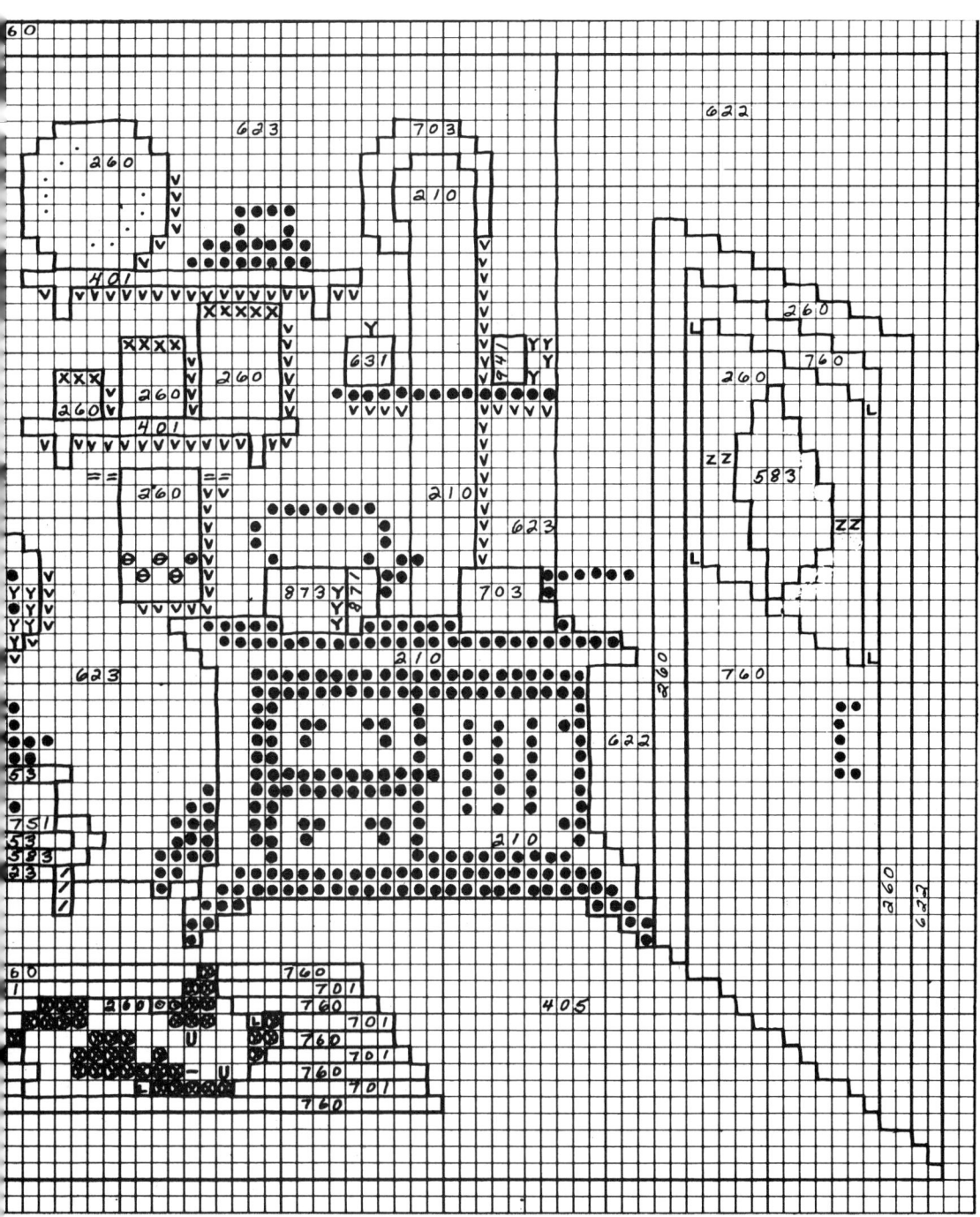

See color chart on page 39.

SYMBOL	PAT. #	COLOR
Ⓞ	760	Light Daffodil Yellow
··	875	Flesh
+	940	Dark Red
X	941	Red
N	943	Dark Pink
Z	944	Medium Pink
−	945	Light Pink

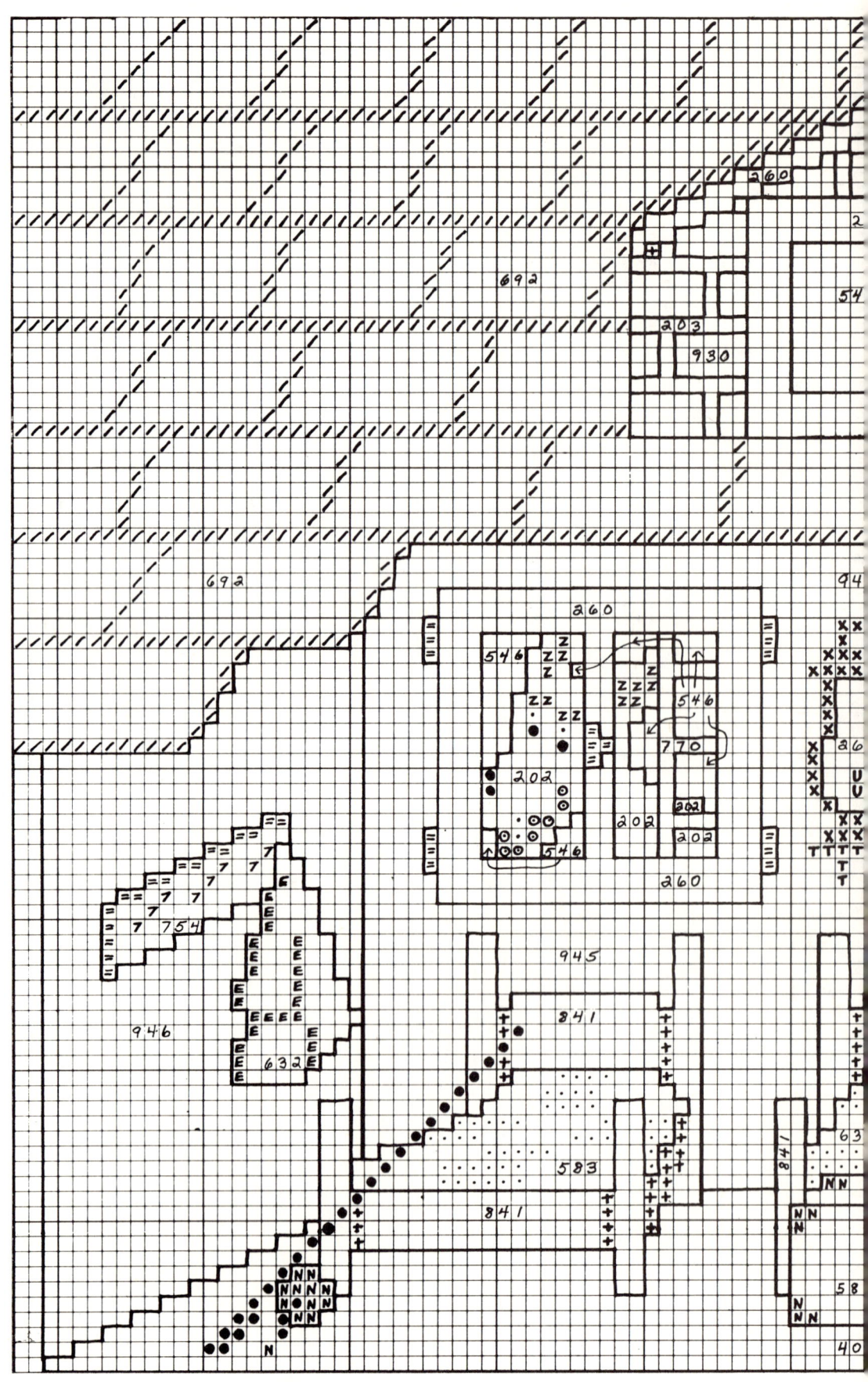

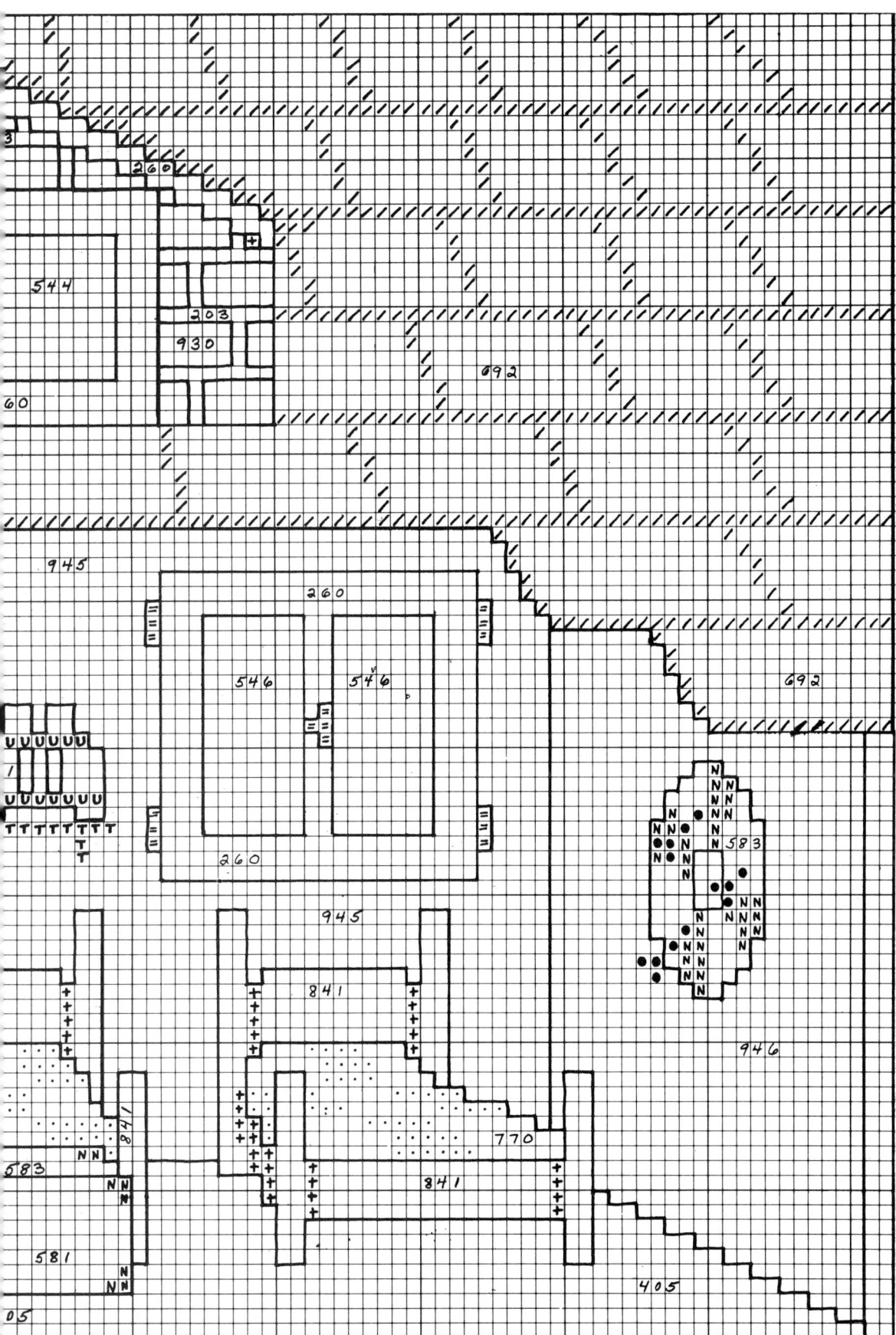

See color chart on page 48 and color key on pages 46–47.

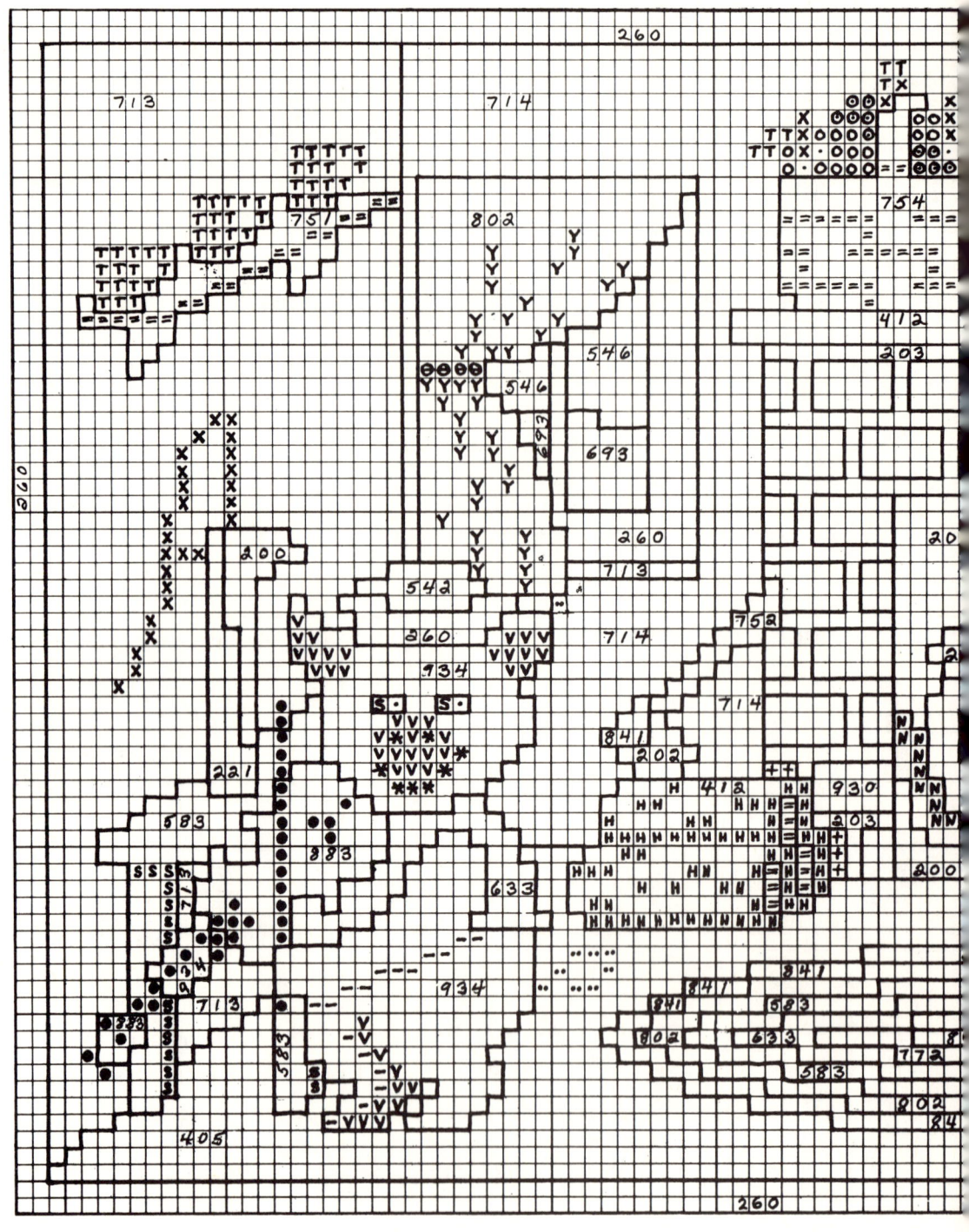

SYMBOL	PAT. #	COLOR
X	221	Charcoal Gray
Z	200	Dark Gray
U	202	Medium Gray
●	220	Black
·	260	White
H	411	Dark Brown

SYMBOL	PAT. #	COLOR
S	581	Dark Sky Blue
●	583	Medium Sky Blue
E	631	Dark Spring Green
T	632	Medium Spring Green
╱	691	Dark Loden Green
7	751	Dark Gold

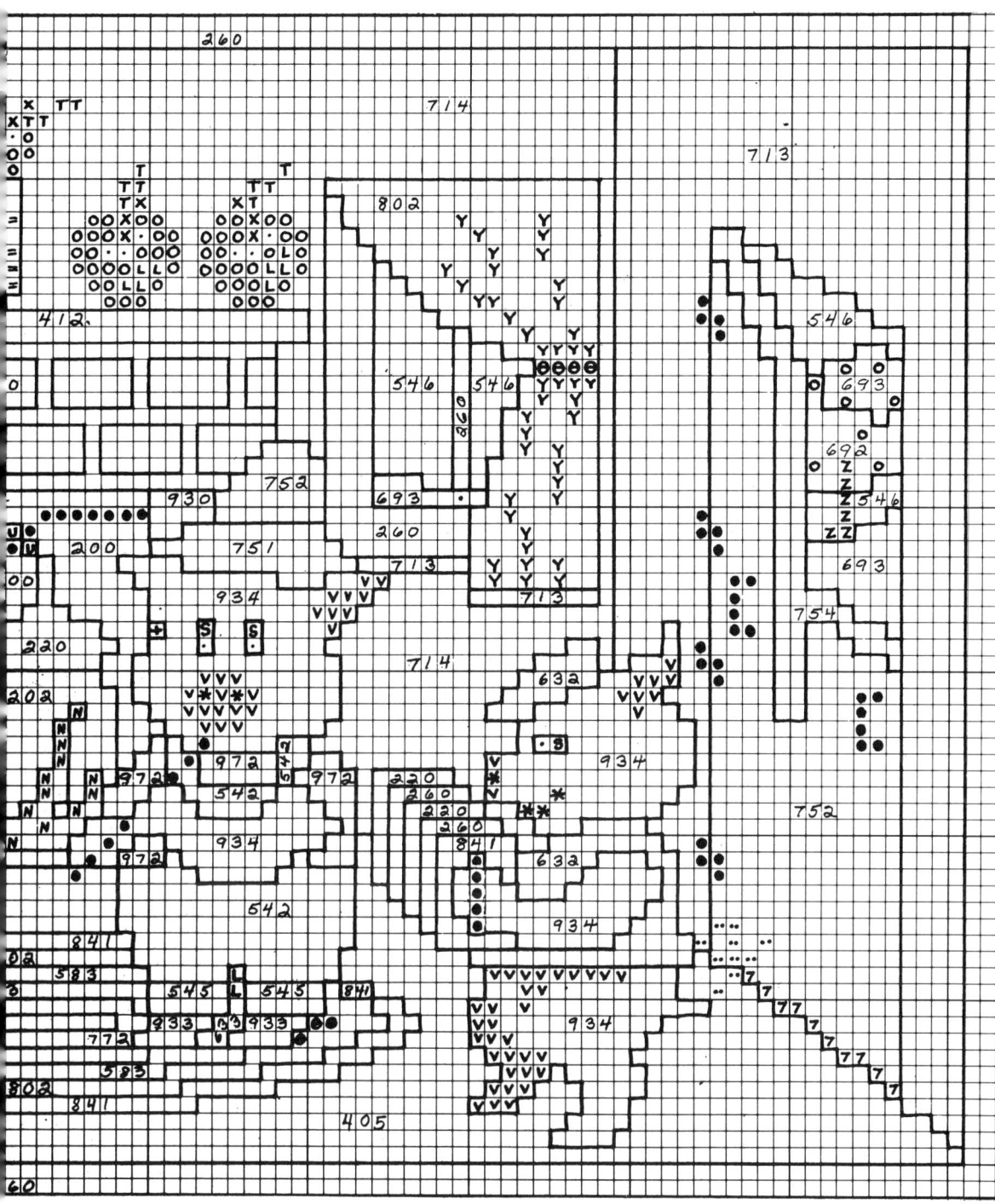

See color chart on page 48.

SYMBOL	PAT. #	COLOR
⊟	752	Medium Gold
N	772	Light Yellow
Y	800	Medium Orange
L	802	Light Orange
◎	840	Dark Red
O	841	Medium Red

SYMBOL	PAT. #	COLOR
⊞	930	Very Dark Pink
✱	931	Dark Pink
V	932	Pink
⊟	933	Light Pink
⠒	934	Pale Pink

The Three Little Pigs
Color Chart

cup shelf	accordion	violin/flute	coat/coat rack	overalls	hats	shirts	pigs	wolf	basket	apples	pump	hearth/fire	rug	firewood/ax	mantel	bricks/mortar	ladder	rod/reel	dart board	binoculars/shelf	lamp	trunk	quilts	beds	door	curtains	tree/grass	windows	dormer window	sky	floors	walls	roof	No.	Color	Category
	×	×						×			×							×	×						×									220	BLACK	
										×	×										×													221	Charcoal	GRAY
								×			×	×															×							200	Dk.	GRAY
								×				×		×						×	×													202	Med.	GRAY
																×																		203	Lt.	GRAY
	×			×				×		×											×	×				×								260	WHITE	
														×																				411	Dk. Brown	BROWN
														×	×																			412	Med. Brown	BROWN
																															×			405	Lt. Brown	BROWN
	×																																	883	Ginger	BROWN
				×	×																													542	Dk. Cobalt	BLUE
																												×						544	Med. Cobalt	BLUE
				×																														545	Lt. Cobalt	BLUE
																														×				546	Pale Cobalt	BLUE
											×										×													581	Dk. Sky Blue	BLUE
											×			×						×	×	×			×									583	Med. Sky Blue	BLUE
×					×						×									×														631	Dk. Spring	GREEN
													×														×							632	Med. Spring	GREEN
														×													×							633	Lt. Spring	GREEN
			×																														×	691	Dk. Loden	GREEN
			×																								×						×	692	Med. Loden	GREEN
																											×							693	Lt. Loden	GREEN
																																×		713	Med. Mustard	YELLOW/ORANGE
																																×		714	Lt. Mustard	YELLOW/ORANGE
×			×	×																														751	Dk. Gold	YELLOW/ORANGE
×			×	×					×					×												×	×							752	Med. Gold	YELLOW/ORANGE
			×						×																	×								754	Lt. Gold	YELLOW/ORANGE
												×						×			×													770	Med. Yellow	YELLOW/ORANGE
												×	×			×		×	×															772	Lt. Yellow	YELLOW/ORANGE
																											×							800	Med. Orange	YELLOW/ORANGE
																											×							802	Lt. Orange	YELLOW/ORANGE
								×		×																								840	Dk. Red	RED
	×									×				×	×											×	×							841	Med. Red	RED
			×																×															972	Lt. Xmas Red	RED
																×									×									930	Very Dk. Pink	PINK
							×																											931	Dk. Pink	PINK
							×																											932	Med. Pink	PINK
							×																											933	Lt. Pink	PINK
							×																											934	Pale Pink	PINK
																																×		945	Med. Cranberry	PINK
																																×		946	Lt. Cranberry	PINK